W9-CAR-608

T. S. ELIOT
THE DESIGN
OF
HIS POETRY

T. S. ELIOT
THE DESIGN
OF HIS
POETRY

BY

Elizabeth Drew

NEW YORK
CHARLES SCRIBNER'S SONS

COPYRIGHT, 1949, BY
CHARLES SCRIBNER'S SONS

———

Printed in the United States of America

B-6.61[MC]

*All rights reserved. No part of this book
may be reproduced in any form without
the permission of Charles Scribner's Sons*

To

John L. Sweeney

ACKNOWLEDGMENTS

The author gratefully acknowledges permission given by Mr. T. S. Eliot and the Master of Eliot House to quote from unpublished material in the Eliot House Collection, Harvard. The quotations throughout the volume from the following works of T. S. Eliot are reprinted by permission of Harcourt, Brace and Company, Inc.: *Collected Poems* 1909-1935, copyright, 1936, by Harcourt, Brace and Company, Inc.; *Four Quartets,* copyright, 1943, by T. S. Eliot; *Selected Essays* 1917-1932, copyright, 1932, by Harcourt, Brace and Company, Inc. The passages from *The Use of Poetry and the Use of Criticism* are reprinted by permission of Harvard University Press, Cambridge, Mass.

The material from the books of Dr. C. G. Jung is quoted by permission of the following publishers: Routledge and Kegan Paul, Ltd.; Baillière Tindall and Cox; Harcourt, Brace and Company, Inc., and Yale University Press.

'Poetry is of course not to be defined by its uses . . . It may effect revolutions in sensibility such as are periodically needed; may help to break up the conventional modes of perception and valuation which are perpetually forming, and make people see the world afresh, or some new part of it. It may make us from time to time a little more aware of the deeper, unnamed feelings which form the substratum of our being, to which we rarely penetrate; for our lives are mostly a constant evasion of ourselves, and an evasion of the visible and sensible world. But to say all this is only to say what you know already, if you have felt poetry and thought about your feelings.'

T. S. Eliot. *The Use of Poetry and the Use of Criticism*

PREFACE

'Criticism must always profess an end in view, which, roughly speaking, appears to be the elucidation of works of art.' This is Eliot's own definition of the function of criticism, in his essay with that title; and it is one with which most people would agree. The elucidation centres in and radiates from a search for *design*, in every meaning of that word. All art springs from the impulse to impose pattern upon experience. Poetry, using the medium of language, seeks to give a living verbal substance and outline to the unorganized feelings, perceptions, ideas and sensations afloat in the personal consciousness of the poet. But any attempt at the elucidation of this process of metamorphosis by which shapeless, untidy, vagrant consciousness becomes what Yeats calls 'proud, living, unwasted words,' brings with it the further awareness that 'a style, a rhythm, to be significant, must embody a significant mind.' Any exploration of the techniques of poetry is inextricably intermingled with the exploration of another element in design, 'the figure in the carpet,' and the attempt to elucidate that. What is the poet *designating* in his pattern of words? How is his mind, through his own particular style and rhythm, making us 'See the world afresh, or some new part of it'? What *designs upon us* does he have? How is he modelling his medium of communication so that through his own patterned sensibility and understanding our own shall be awakened and shaped?

The elucidation of works of art, then, becomes an effort at the interpretations of these inter-related patterns. The critic or teacher or reader is fully aware that his search for 'meaning,' and his own expression of a poem's 'meaning' exists in a very restricted and very different order of being from that of the work of art itself, which remains proud, living and unwasteful in its assertion of its own vitality. But just as the creation of poetry is the result of a compulsion towards expression

and communication, so a similar compulsion visits its readers.
Eliot himself admits the presence of what he calls this 'restless
demon' and its drive.

> Our impulse to interpret a work of art (by 'work
> of art' I mean here rather the work of one artist as a
> whole) is exactly as imperative and fundamental as our
> impulse to interpret the universe by metaphysics . . .
> and Bradley's apothegm that 'metaphysics is the find-
> ing of bad reasons for what we believe upon instinct;
> but to find these reasons is no less an instinct'; applies
> as precisely to the interpretation of poetry. . . . To
> interpret then, or to seek to pounce upon the secret, to
> elucidate the pattern and pluck out the mystery of a
> poet's work, is 'no less an instinct.' Nor is the effort al-
> together vain; for as the study of philosophy, and
> indeed the surrendering ourselves . . . to some system
> of our own or of someone else, is as needful part of a
> man's life as falling in love or making any contract,
> so is it necessary to surrender ourselves to some inter-
> pretation of the poetry we like.

This passage is from Eliot's preface to *The Wheel of Fire* by
G. Wilson Knight, a book which explores Shakespeare's poetic
symbols and imagery. Any critic of Eliot's poetry inevitably
sets out on a similar exploration. I have found what is, to
me, an interesting parallel in symbolic content between the
progression of dream symbols described by Jung as arising
during what he calls 'the integration of the personality' (and
which he relates to the history of myth), and some of those
appearing in Eliot's poetry during the course of its development.[1] But this is not a book about rival schools of psychology
and anthropology.. I have very little knowledge of either, and
am in no way qualified to judge them. Moreover any approach
to poetry through psychology seems to me to be blocked very

---

[1] My interest in this was first aroused by an article on *The Archetypal
Imagery of T. S. Eliot* by Genevieve W. Foster in *PMLA.*, Vol. 60
[1945], 567-585.

early. Psychology can suggest a good deal about the unconscious forces at work behind the conception of art, but it has
limitations which make it a very poor critical instrument. It
cannot touch the work of art itself, and it cannot distinguish between good art and bad. The mere presence of certain images
in poetry, therefore, though it may be of psychological interest,
has nothing to do with its vitality. The life of poetry springs
from the inter-relationships of words in a formal pattern. It is
from an exploration of those that elucidation must start.

But these inter-relationships are more than usually complex in the poetry of Eliot. An analysis of them requires us to
'break up conventional modes of perception and valuation,'
and an exploration of them soon leads us to those 'deeper,
unnamed feelings which form the substratum of our being, to
which we rarely penetrate.' So that both new insights and a
new way of arriving at insights are included in Eliot's designs.
There is, to alter Wordsworth's image, a film of unfamiliarity
in the reader's eye which must be dispersed before he can see
what the poetry is doing.

A large body of criticism already exists dealing with the
sources of his literary allusions, with various aspects of his
symbolic method, and with the elucidation of certain individual
poems. To this I am deeply indebted. There has, however, been
no attempt to write of the body of the poetry as a process of
growth, as an 'integration of the personality.' The particular
purpose of this book is to do that, and to help the general
reader, and the student, to a fuller enjoyment of the individual
poems by analysis and discussion. Any such analyses must be
open to attack. All interpretation must be personal and partial,
and as Marianne Moore said: 'Expanded explanation tends
to spoil the lion's leap.' But any newcomer to the critics of
Eliot is in good company as he yields to that 'restless demon'
with its 'imperative and fundamental impulse.' And we may
add another simple statement by Eliot himself: 'Our talking
about poetry is a part of, an extension of, our experience of it.'

CONTENTS

T. S. ELIOT
THE DESIGN
OF
HIS POETRY

CHAPTER I

◆◆◆

The Mythical Vision

In looking at objects of Nature, I seem rather to be
seeking, as it were *asking* for, a symbolical language for
something within me that already and for ever exists,
than observing anything new.

S. T. COLERIDGE

'I hold this book to be the most important expression
which the present age has found . . . In using the myth,
in manipulating a continuous parallel between contemporaneity and antiquity, Mr. Joyce is pursuing a method
which others must pursue after him. They will not be
imitators, any more than the scientist who uses the discoveries of an Einstein in pursuing his own, independent,
further investigations. It is simply a way of controlling,
of ordering, of giving a shape and a significance to the
immense panorama of futility and anarchy which is contemporary history . . . It is a method for which the
horoscope is auspicious. Psychology (such as it is, and
whether our reaction to it be comic or serious), ethnology
and *The Golden Bough* have concurred to make possible
what was impossible even a few years ago. Instead of
narrative method, we may now use the mythical method.
It is, I seriously believe, a step towards making the modern
world possible for art, towards . . . order and form. And
only those who have won their own discipline in secret
and without aid, in a world which offers very little assistance to that end, can be of any use in furthering this
advance.'[1]

[1] *The Dial.* November, 1923.

1

The whole tone of this passage from Eliot's review of *Ulysses* suggests that in it he is not merely commenting on an interesting and original work by a fellow literary artist, but that there is something in the method of the creation of that work which has excited him profoundly; that it contains some revelation of wide and deep significance for himself and for others. He likens its importance to that of the most revolutionary discoveries in the physical universe, and his mind jumps for an analogy to the ancient belief that linked man's fate with the courses of the stars. As an astrologer of old plotted the encompassing position of the constellations to discover the controlling forces of a particular future, and rejoiced to find them favourable, so Eliot sees the happiest future for art under the influence of a new controlling factor. He calls this 'the mythical method' and he sees it as a way by which the artist can give shape and significance to the chaotic material of contemporary life. He can set the 'immense panorama of futility and anarchy' in opposition to the pattern of a different vision; he can 'manipulate a parallel' with the world of myth.

But the stories of ancient mythology have always been a source of inspiration to the literary artist, as their use in every age has amply shown. What then does Eliot mean when he says that recent discoveries in anthropology and psychology have made the mythical method possible, and that it is the most important expression the present age has found?

He means that modern explorations of myth have changed completely the conceptions of its origins, its nature and its function. Myth (the etymological root is the same as that of *mystery*) leads us back to ultimate mysteries, not only the mystery of life itself, but of that element in life by which man differentiated himself from the rest of the animal creation: speech. *Mythos* meant 'word,' and the development of man's use of the term from *mythos* to *epos* to *logos* is itself the story of his developing use of language; from the word meaning a symbolic reflection of his earliest consciousness; to the word meaning a structure of events in time; to the word meaning a pattern of rational values.

Modern scholarship now recognizes that myth is no dead form, a relic of antiquity, an empty survival. It is true that the ancient stories we call 'myths' are primitive legends expressing man's first response to his world, but the *manner* of that response springs from a faculty alive in all ages of man's existence. The mythical method is the presentation of experience in symbolic form, the earliest and still the most direct and immediate form of human expression. Long before man developed the power of logical discourse and intellectual interpretation, the material transmitted to his mind through his senses moulded itself into meaning in myth. The outer worlds of physical nature, of human character, action and endeavour, and the inner world of his own conscious and unconscious response to these things, formed themselves in him, and were in turn formed and developed *by* him into symbolic configurations, into metaphorical conceptions and expressions. It was the first step of primitive man 'towards order and form'; the giving of imaginative shape and significance to the totality of his experience.

And since its aim was to encompass his experience in its wholeness, to communicate his sense of the revelation of its meaning, primitive myth always creates a pattern in which man brings himself into significant relationship with mysterious forces outside the actualities of his daily life. He senses himself as part of a symbolic drama extending far beyond himself. Anthropologists now trace all the symbolic formulations of primitive myth and religion, and of the ritual inseparable from them, to the primeval consciousness of a magic or *mana* potency indwelling in the physical universe and accessible to man, though forever evading his practical understanding:

> In the case of any important magic we invariably find the story accounting for its existence. Such a story tells when and where it entered the possession of man.

But it is not the story of its origins. Magic has never been made or invented. All magic simply 'was' from the beginning an essential adjunct of all such things and processes as vitally interest man and yet elude his normal rational efforts.[2]

Myth, therefore, was the symbolic presentation of primitive man's instinct that his work-a-day-world was interpenetrated with a super-rational or extra-rational activity in which he himself could and did share. There was an anonymous source of vitality diffused throughout the universe and in himself, which he objectified in dramatic symbols and so made operative in human experience. His myths were fabulous fictions which revealed psychic facts: they were images which intensified and expanded and gave grandeur of design to his existence. Through them he became part of a unity composed of two activities. On the one hand he appeared merely a social unit in the common round of diurnal enterprise, but he apprehended too a symbolic drama where that apparently planless flux of being and becoming related itself to changeless patterns of creative and destructive forces; patterns of value, existing on a different plane of living, and requiring a language of their own.

He created this symbolic drama in that language, the language of myth and ritual, which thus became the heritage of the race handed on from generation to generation. Through it the individual and the tribe were alike united with the indestructible potencies symbolized, and brought into close and purposive relation with them. Thus the function of myth and ritual in the primitive community was the creation of expressive forms which satisfied man's primeval need of spiritual reassurance and social stability. The myth vouched for the 'magic' that was alive in the universe, while the ritual asso-

---

[2] 'Magic, Science & Religion,' Bronislaw Malinowski, in *Science, Religion & Reality,* edited by Joseph Needham, London. The Sheldon Press, 1926, p. 69.

ciated with the sacred tradition defeated the destructive aspects of the 'magic' and transmitted its beneficent powers into the life of the individual and the tribe. The formal rite concentrated and channeled the cosmic energies, disposing their strength and value directly upon the affairs of men.

Modern anthropology sees all religion and all art springing and growing from this primitive root of symbolic transformation. By his symbol-making instinct man's knowledge and experience of the outer and inner world were projected into direct sensuous embodiment, giving them life and outline and meaning, turning force into form. And it was the juxtaposition of the 'shape and significance' of life given expression in these symbolic terms with 'the immense panorama of futility and anarchy which is contemporary history' in which Eliot saw a hope for a new advance towards order and form.

The contribution of psychology to that possibility has been to explore behind the *results* of man's symbol-making instincts and needs, to their source in his own being. Though psychology has come to no verifiable conclusions about the origins or the nature of the source, it has done much to clarify both its workings and its functions. It has also given it a name and called it 'the unconscious,' that part of the psyche which Jung describes as 'the eternally creative mother of consciousness; the never failing source of all art and of all human productivity.' To the psychologist, the 'magic' which to the primitive just 'was', originates in the unconscious, whence man projects it upon the external world, endowing physical objects or his self-made symbolic figures with properties and behaviour from its own reality; giving psychic life from its own energies to the objects of its wonder, fear, love, hate, reverence or contempt.

Freud, at his seventieth birthday celebration, refused credit for the discovery of the unconscious. That, he said, properly belonged to the masters of literature, who had always been aware of its presence, its pressures and its powers. Jung would agree with him. But the two great psychological pioneers of the contemporary world parted company over the question of the derivation of myth. Though both agree it has its root in the unconscious and the strange phenomenon of the dream image, they differ radically in their theories and interpretations of its genesis.

To Freud, the scientific positivist, the unconscious contents of the human psyche consist solely of material suppressed by the conscious. To him the unconscious is a pathological or infantile activity of the mind and the disguised symbols of mythological situation which arise in it mere symptoms of these all-prevailing but basically unhealthy suppressions. He sees all myth, all religion and all art as originating in such suppressions. Moreover, although the resulting symbolic manifestations are so complex and so varied, their originating cause is simple: 'the beginnings of religion, ethics, society and art meet in the Oedipus complex.' [3] He interprets all unconscious drives exclusively in sexual and familial terms, and their emergence into myth and ritual as illustrating various aspects of the ambivalent emotions of love and hate, admiration and fear, attraction and repulsion, inherent in the parent-child relationship. 'In the beginning was the deed,' [4] the original murder (whether in imagination or in actuality) of the primal father, springing from the incest motive, and all further developments of mythical legend and religious ritual are transpositions and releases into acceptable terms of the repressed emotional forces occasioned by that ever-recurring central situation in the life of the individual.

To Jung, however, this theory very early appeared inadequate. He could not square the tremendous dynamic effects of mythic-religious concepts on man's history, art and behaviour with a belief that their symbolic origin was morbid

[3] *Totem & Tabu,* p. 260.
[4] *Ibid.,* p. 268.

or that they derived solely from experience in the single individual life. He felt that such psychic happenings could not be explained *away* in other terms, but must be explained as psychic events with an independent nature of their own. He became convinced that the symbols generated in dream from the unconscious sprang not only from man as a disordered object, but also from a level of his psychic activity where his faculty of symbolic transformation made him a self-creating subject.

It is clear that such a conception of the activities of the human psyche would be more congenial to Eliot as a contribution to the 'mythical method' than the theories of Freud. In his remarks on *Ulysses,* however, Eliot injects parentheses after his mention of psychology—'(such as it is and whether our reaction to it be comic or serious).' In *The Dry Salvages* he appears to class it with fortune-telling, palmistry and astrology as 'pastimes and drugs.' He is, however, kinder elsewhere:

> Psychology has very great utility in two ways. It can revive, and has already to some extent revived, truths long since known to Christianity, but mostly forgotten and ignored, and it can put them in a form and a language understandable by modern people to whom the language of Christianity is not only dead but undecipherable . . . But I must add that I think psychology can do more than this, in discovering more about the human soul still; for I do not pretend that there is nothing more to know; the possibilities of knowledge are practically endless. Psychology is an indispensable handmaid to theology; but I think a very poor housekeeper.[5]

But in spite of this 'serious' reaction to the subject, the core of the criticism is in the last sentence, and it is obvious that it was not through psychology that Eliot reached his own

[5] *The Listener.* March 30, 1932.

conclusions about the nature of reality. Yet apart from such ultimate problems, the development of his poetry contains an interesting parallel to some of the materials cited by Jung, and a confirmation of his belief that certain archetypal patterns of imagery which recur and interfuse in the myths of the human race are of great significance in the problem of the nature of the symbolizing process, as well as that of the nature of life in general.

To Jung these archetypal patterns inhabit a psychic territory which he has called the 'collective unconscious,' an area beyond the personal unconscious first defined scientifically by Freud, and much vaster. It is not altogether clear in what terms Jung regards the collective unconscious. He speaks of it sometimes as a working hypothesis; sometimes as a kind of mighty metaphor (similar to Yeats' 'Great Memory') which images the permanent sameness of man's deepest psychic patterns. It would surely seem as if it belongs in this category, where it could be generally accepted as of very great interest and enlightenment in the exploration of all the great recurring themes of myth and literature. But Jung, while admitting that evidences of it are to be found only in particular individuals, seems often to accept it as having universal scope as fact.

> There is no reason for believing that the psyche, with its peculiar structure, is the only thing in the world that has no history behind its individual manifestations. Even the conscious mind cannot be denied a history extending over at least five thousand years. It is only individual ego-consciousness that has forever a new beginning and an early end. But the unconscious psyche is not only immensely old, it is also able to grow unceasingly into an equally remote future. It forms, and is part of, the human species just as much as the body, which is also individually ephemeral, yet collectively of immeasurable duration.[6]

[6] *The Integration of the Personality*, p. 25.

Just as tradition is the inherited wisdom of the race consciously expressed, so Jung envisages the collective unconscious as the *un*conscious inherited wisdom of the race. As such he sees it as accounting not only for the striking analogies between the themes and patterns of myth in many different cultures, but also for the presence of recurring mythological and archaic symbols in dreams, even in the dreams of those who have no knowledge of the traditional and literary sources which perpetuate them.

It is to these symbols that Jung has given the name of *archetypes* or *primordial images,* and he sees them not only as the raw materials from which the myths and religions of the race have been consciously elaborated, but as constantly recurring revelations of creative and destructive potentialities in the individual. They appear as symbols in man's deepest inner conflicts, in which his most vital energies are brought into play and 'they become accessible to consciousness only in the presence of that degree of self-awareness and power of understanding which enables a man to think what he experiences instead of just living it blindly.' [7] In fact, just as tradition is meaningless unless its continuity is also a process of continual recreation in society and in the individual, so with this racial memory. Its images, to be of any value, must be recreated in collaboration with the conscious intelligence into a process of ordered growth. Just as the language of myth and ritual gave significant pattern to tribal tradition and so satisfied the needs of primitive man for inner communal security, so Jung sees the same process accomplished for modern man through the conscious adaptation of these symbolic messages from the unconscious into richer patterns of individual living.

Moreover not only do they make him aware of the character of the eternally recurring conflicts to be resolved, but they are actual instruments of the resolution. Jung not only postulates the *presence* of the racial memory, of these deposits of inherited

[7] *Psychological Types,* p. 272.

psychic experience which in certain circumstances and in certain temperaments can become stirred and active, but his experience has led him to detect in them not only a peculiarly powerful dynamism, but a *purposive* quality of their own. At the other extreme from Freud's belief that such dream images are relics of primitive and infantile modes of reaction, blocking the way to the mature development of the ego, Jung regards them as revelations of psychic potentialities, 'the mighty spiritual inheritance of human development, reborn in every individual.' When particular circumstances are encountered in the life of the individual which bring him into touch with some aspect of this universal collective experience, the images appear, modified by the personal circumstances and sensibilities of the dreamer, but bringing with them always the peculiarly stirring and energizing sense of involvement in larger and more impersonal forces.

> Each of these images contains a piece of human psychology and human destiny, a relic of suffering or delight that has happened countless times in our ancestral story, and on the average follows ever in the same course. It is like a deeply graven river-bed in the soul, in which the waters of life, that had spread hitherto with groping and uncertain course over wide but shallow surfaces, suddenly become a mighty river. This happens when that particular chain of circumstances is encountered which from immemorial time has contributed to the laying down of the primordial image. The moment when the mythological situation appears is always characterized by a peculiar emotional intensity; it is as though chords in us were touched that had never resounded before, or as though forces were unloosed, the existence of which we had never dreamed.[8]

And to Jung, not only are the forces unloosed, but the

---

[8] 'On the Relation of Analytical Psychology to Poetic Art,' *Contributions to Analytical Psychology*, p. 247.

symbols through which they reveal themselves have a peculiar-ly compelling power. It is as if the individual were agent and interpreter of something which is as it were shaping *him* and being shaped *by* him in a reciprocal action. For in the incessant flux of lively antagonisms and perpetual oppositions which sustain the energies of psychic vitality, Jung detects an inner ordering principle, a purposive process, as compulsive as that of physical growth itself. Though he does not pretend to know what 'spirit' is, he insists on it as a force in its own right. He will not accept the 'spiritual' as a derivative of sex, even in the widest application of that term. 'The spiritual appears in the psyche likewise as a drive, indeed as a true passion. It is no derivative of another drive, but the indispensable formative power in the world of drives.' To those who become aware of this drive, this true passion, the archetypes and primordial images can act in the nature of energy transformers. They absorb and resolve the opposing charges on which the pur-posive use of psychic force depend and the fresh energy thus released can be directed towards future development.

In such cases it is as if the individual were himself caught up into the world of myth, made living instead of legendary, and with the content of its conscious and unconscious dramatic material revealed gradually as a creative process. And being in a sense artist too as well as a character in the drama, con-trolling as well as being controlled by the symbolic forms; be-ing able 'to think what he experiences instead of just living it blindly,' the individual has the power to collaborate consciously in the design. He waits for those moments when fabulous fiction explodes into psychic fact; when seemingly unrelated and ambiguous symbols constellate into pattern; when many-faceted 'meaning' resolves itself from apparently irreconcilable paradox. Thus the material from the conscious and the un-conscious situation 'given' symbolically in the dream image is reduced by the conscious formative process to new contours and compounds of thought and action. The *mythos* of the symbol itself is united to the *epos* of action and to the *logos* of constructive thought.

There are as many archetypes as there are figures and situations in myth, for to Jung the psyche contains all the images that have ever given rise to myths. He has analyzed a great number of them in his own terms of interpretation,[9] but there is one particular 'constellation of primordial images' to which he repeatedly returns in his writings, and which he regards as the accompaniment of the central psychic adventure of mature human life. He refers to the whole experience under the general title of 'the archetype of transformation' and in non-symbolic language as the process of Individuation or the Integration of the Personality. It is the experience of detachment from the world of objective reality as the centre of existence and the finding of 'a new dimension' in which it can and must be contemplated and lived. Detachment too from the ego as the centre of interest and the discovery of a different centre. As such it involves the process of the death of an old life and the birth of a new, the process traced back by Frazer and other scholars as the inner meaning of the symbolism of the oldest Fertility rituals, and the basis of their development into tragic drama. It is the paradox expressed in the pattern of *Oedipus Rex*. There, in the scene where Oedipus begins that exploration of the truth which will shatter his whole framework of temporal prosperity, the seer Tiresias says: 'This day shall give you birth and death.' It appears in innumerable forms in myth and legend, and is, of course, inseparably intertwined with the whole symbolic content of Christianity. 'Except a corn of wheat fall into the ground

[9] See particularly *The Psychology of the Unconscious*, which contains his own theory of the meaning of the 'Oedipus complex.'

and die, it abideth alone: but if it die, it bringeth forth much fruit': 'Except a man be born of water and of the spirit he cannot enter into the Kingdom of God': 'Whosoever will save his life shall lose it.'

During the process of 'transformation,' as observed psychologically by Jung, certain archetypal images regularly occur, forming a continuity and interaction of symbols expressing the disintegration and death of the old pattern and the gradual emergence of a new order. When this has established itself, the centre of the personality has been shifted from the ego to a hypothetical point of equilibrium between the individual consciousness and the collective psyche. Rather confusingly Jung calls this point the 'Self' and he says it is

> 'Sensed as an indefinable state of being to which the ego is neither opposed nor subjected, but is in a relation of dependence and around which it revolves, very much as the earth rotates about the sun. I use the word 'sensed' in order to indicate the apperceptive character of the relation between the ego and the Self. In this relation there is nothing knowable in the intellectual sense, because we can say nothing of the contents of the Self. The ego is the only content of the Self that we know. The individuated ego experiences the fact that it is object of an unknown and superordinated subject . . . Visualizations are never more than awkward attempts of a fumbling mind to give some kind of form to the inexpressible psychological facts.' [10]

Of the whole progression he concludes: 'As to what these processes consist in, I have no theory to offer. One would first have to know what the psyche is.' And he thinks that the natural history of the mind is no further advanced today than was the natural science of the thirteenth century.

[10] *Two Essays on Analytical Psychology*, p. 268.

The central experience which informs most of the poetry of Eliot is this same age-old pattern of symbolic death and birth, lived through as an intense personal experience and accepted as the central truth of a religious faith. The Anglican Church to which he belongs has its own historic archetypes and rituals, containing in themselves a complete symbolic ordering of the theme, and, by abstraction in theology, the whole conceptual ordering of the psychic material involved. But Eliot in his poetry does not often use traditional Catholic symbolism. His 'transformations' are all his own in his reliving of the inner reality of the myth. It is of course obvious that without any hypothesis of a collective unconscious, the 'primordial' character of many of his dominating symbols can be accounted for very easily by his saturation in literary tradition. But the *sequence* in which the archetypal images arise in the course of his poetry, their inter-relationships, and their final resolution into the design of *Four Quartets,* reflects in a strange way the succession in the appearance of the symbols which Jung has described as the archetype of transformation. The final development of the images too is in a 'sensing' of a pattern of vital relationships between the ego and a larger order, which arranges itself into the same kind of symbolic design. In this design 'reality' is felt to inhere, though apprehended only through 'hints and guesses.'

This is interesting psychologically, though, if the parallel be valid, it is only a confirming of Jung's hypothesis and not a 'discovering more about the human soul still.' The symbols will be discussed more fully when they begin to emerge in the poems themselves. Meanwhile, to get back to Eliot's review of *Ulysses,* it was not any special symbolic *content* that he was discussing there, but the mythical *method;* myth as illustrating the direct presentation of experience in symbolic form. He was emphasizing Joyce's use of this to manipulate a parallel between past and present. Eliot himself does that specifically in

The Waste Land, but he had been using the method in its general meaning long before. The recognition of sensuous symbolism as the richest form of human perception, and its ordering into pattern as the basis of poetic technique, had been from the beginning his whole theory and practice of poetry.

CHAPTER II

❖

The Mythical Method

The artist, I believe, is more primitive, as well as more civilized, than his contemporaries; his experience is deeper than civilization, and he only uses the phenomena of civilization in expressing it.

(T. S. ELIOT. Review of *Tarr* by Wyndham Lewis. *The Egoist,* September, 1918.)

His language is not, like the language of bad poetry, dead. It is very much alive, with this singular life of its own. But the language which is more important to us is that which is struggling to digest and express new objects, new groups of objects, new feelings, new aspects. . . .

T. S. ELIOT. *Swinburne as Poet* (1920)

Eliot wrote at the end of his review of *Ulysses* that it was only those who had won their discipline in secret and without aid, in a world which offered very little assistance to that end, who could be of any use in furthering the development of the 'mythical method.' We cannot doubt that the author of the early poems and of the critical essays in *The Sacred Wood,* who had published *The Waste Land* in the year preceding the appearance of *Ulysses,* knew himself to be one of these. We look, therefore, in his early poetry and criticism for the statement and illustration of the qualities which he regarded as the necessary training for his task.

With the expansion of his own interests and his own practice, Eliot has modified, or developed rather, some of his earlier critical dogma.

16

The poet, when he talks or writes about poetry, has peculiar qualifications and peculiar limitations . . . I can never reread any of my own prose writings without acute embarrassment . . . But I believe that the critical writings of poets . . . owe a great deal of their interest to the fact that at the back of the poet's mind, if not as his ostensible purpose, he is always trying to defend the kind of poetry he is writing, or to formulate the kind that he wants to write. Especially when he is young, and actively engaged in battling for the kind of poetry which he practises, he sees the poetry of the past in relation to his own . . . When he theorizes about poetic creation, he is likely to be generalizing one type of experience; when he ventures into aesthetics, he is likely to be less, rather than more competent than the philosophers; and he may do best to report, for the information of the philosophers, the data of his own introspection. What he writes about poetry, in short, must be assessed in relation to the poetry he writes.[1]

At the outset of his career, however, Eliot was an active rebel and revolutionary, and his purpose, in both poetry and criticism, was to direct attention towards the particular sources of poetic power whose neglect had led, he felt, to a progressive devitalization of the practice of poetic art. He traced this not only to the general loss of the sense of tradition, but to the specific loss of direct symbolic transformation as a method of perception. The primitive mythmaker, for example, did not analyze or describe in terms of logical discourse, the idea that human life is fertilized by forces from the worlds of nature and of spirit. Instead, he embodied his consciousness of that truth in the myth of Leda ravished by Zeus in the form of a swan. The idea lives through the sensuous embodiment of it and in the sensations aroused by that. From those we abstract the 'thought' that man is body, a part of the natural world, and union with nature is one source of his being; but there is a

---

[1] *The Music of Poetry*. Partisan Review. November-December 1942.

power beyond that of nature, for which, however, he can find an image only *in* nature. It comes *like* a great bird in flight from the sky; the inflowing of its vital force is *like* the act by which man fertilizes woman. It is violent and joyous, and its product is Helen of Troy—beauty inspiring passions which hold the seeds of both creation and destruction, love and war.

That method of perceiving inner realities *through* their reflection in concrete image, and all the disciplines which have to accompany its translation into language, was what Eliot was in particular 'battling to recapture' in the practice of poetry. He saw the source of power in this symbolic concentration dissipated, and the language of poetry rendered weak and flaccid by the substitution of the 'narrative method,' or by what he describes elsewhere as 'rumination.' He saw poetry given over to description, to discussion, to reflection or to mere decoration, while the readers of poetry too became habituated to receive their experience of poetry in those ways. They had come to expect explanation instead of revelation; to expect a method by which thought and emotion and sensation were elaborated as separate entities, each adding its quota to the whole, and related in a process of extended verbal clarification. Eliot wanted to recapture all the concentration which the symbol brings as a result of the kind of perception in which object and 'meaning' synchronize and are recognized simultaneously. And not a single 'meaning,' since no symbol can ever be pinned down to that. As it embodies both thought and sensation, so all the potential proliferation of physical life itself, and all the *relating* qualities of thinking, live in it together. It is body and mind in one: it both means and is. It has 'shape and significance;' a sensuous body and a 'meaning' which points beyond body. It is complete in itself and yet life, inward and outward life, are not only contained in it, but flow from it in every direction. It was to bring back this unruly life-force into poetry, and to rule it by the discipline of poetic form, for which Eliot fought: to capture and communicate the rich mythic quality of perception in the ritual of words.

For the poet's medium is language and it is only through words that the quality of his thinking and feeling become operative. Here too, Eliot was intuitively alive to those links with the primitive which bind the poet to the history of the race. Poetry had its origin in ritual incantation and dance. We still speak of the spell of poetry, of its magic and enchantment, as a metaphorical term, but to our primitive ancestors it was a reality; the word had power over the thing. The utterance of the magic formulas, charged with the potency of tradition, released that power into the immediate present. At the same time, the formal ceremonious dance and chant isolated the participants from the fragmentary mundane rhythms of their daily occupations, opening pathways to the inward and secret rhythms of the deeper sources of life. Through the active co-operation of the whole body in the rite, the sense of its inter-inanimating forces was intensified; and at the same time the harmonizing properties of those forces had their counterpart in the ordered response and dramatic decorum of tone and gesture.

Of all this the modern poet is left with the rhythm of his words alone. It is true that the 'phenomena of civilization,' the immense accretion of his verbal material, lend him powers of expression infinitely more complex and subtle, yet the primitive springs of poetry in sound and movement are emphasized by Eliot in *The Music of Poetry*. 'I know that a poem, or a passage in a poem, may tend to realize itself first as a particular rhythm before it reaches expression in words, and that this rhythm may bring to birth the idea and the image; and I do not believe that this is an experience peculiar to myself.' Or again his remarks on the 'auditory imagination' illustrate very well the wealth of significance that he feels to be alive in the whole aural element of the poet's art.

What I call the 'auditory imagination' is the feeling for syllable and rhythm, penetrating far below the conscious levels of thought and feeling, invigorating every word; sinking to the most primitive and forgotten, returning to the origin and bringing something back, seeking the beginning and the end. It works through meanings, certainly, or not without meanings in the ordinary sense, and fuses the old and obliterated and the trite, the current, and the new and surprising, the most ancient and the most civilized mentality.[2]

The keyword in that passage, is that the auditory imagination *fuses;* and as we have seen, it is the experience of fusion, of division and multiplicity reduced to unity, which is the essence of the symbolic or mythical method of grasping experience. The rational and the extra-rational, the old and the new, the primitive and the civilized, thought and feeling, intuition and sensation, blend and are communicated in poetry through the control and manipulation of language. In his essay on *Tradition and the Individual Talent* Eliot gives some account of the poetic process. The poet's mind, he says, is 'a receptacle for seizing and storing up numberless feelings, phrases, images, which remain there until all the particles which can unite to form a new compound are present together.' Their convergence is unconscious and cannot be commanded; there must be 'a passive attending upon the event.' From the moment of 'event,' however, the process turns into active venture, and the poet's whole attention is focussed on the means of his communication, on the further fusion of the materials into a pattern of words. And here again it is the third stage in the process of concentration which is the heart of the matter: it is 'the intensity of the artistic process, the pressure, so to speak, under which the fusion takes place, that counts.' This involves 'frightful toil' and 'a prolonged manipulation of the materials,' which is alto-

[2] *The Use of Poetry and the Use of Criticism,* pp. 118-9.

gether conscious and deliberate: 'probably indeed, the larger part of the labour of an author in composing his work is critical labour; the labour of sifting, combining, constructing, expunging, correcting, testing.' [3]

Speaking of the 'exaggerated repute' of *Kubla Khan,* Eliot points out that this is the process which has there been omitted.

> The imagery of that fragment, certainly, whatever its origin in Coleridge's reading, sank to the depths of Coleridge's feeling, was saturated, transformed there— 'those are pearls that were his eyes'—and brought up into daylight again. But it is not *used*: the poem has not been written . . . Organisation is necessary as well as 'inspiration.' [4]

Organisation is a forbidding word on the face of it, yet its implications are very wide and rich. It links life with order, bringing the useful reminder that all life *is* order, and that in every field it is a matter of relationships and reconciliations. A poem is an organism, composed of living parts separate in function yet mutually dependent; where everything is used and fused. Its force springs from the process of interpenetration, which is its organisation. That is its 'technique,' but as Eliot says: 'we cannot say where technique begins and ends.' Matter and manner are a new body-mind indivisibility. A process of collision and collusion takes place, by which the 'particles' cohere to form a new whole. The fragmentary experiences of feeling and thinking which are those of life and reading take on a different kind of vitality and value, that of a poem. It is a process in which obscure, confused and dispersed features and members take on a unique and living form and are held together in a single field of force: a process by which

---

[3] 'The Function of Criticism,' *Selected Essays*, p. 30.
[4] *The Use of Poetry and the Use of Criticism*, p. 146.

the flesh is made word, impersonalized in the passionate pre-occupation of 'turning blood into ink,' and materialized again into a new concentration of outline and energy; given a new body.

The emphasis which Eliot's theory and practice lays on the impersonality of art, on the disciplines necessary to it, and on the absorption of the 'idea' into the sensuous embodiment of image and rhythm, reveals at once how alien he felt his own position to be from any ideal of poetry which would describe it as either a 'spontaneous over-flow of powerful feelings' or as a 'criticism of life.' The Romantic and Victorian models, which were the popular ones in England and America when he began to write, gave him no help whatever: 'I do not think it is too sweeping to say that there was no poet, in either country, who could have been of use to a beginner in 1908. The only recourse was to poetry of another age and to poetry of another language.' [5]

It was to the Jacobean dramatists and the French nineteenth century Symbolists that Eliot turned for the kinds of perception and the techniques of expressing them akin to his own creative instincts. There he found what he was seeking. The Symbolists held as the central doctrine of their poetic creed that poetry must transmute life into a new incarnation of image and rhythm. The Jacobean dramatists did it more instinctively. It was their natural way of writing; they were inheritors of a wealth of fresh consciousness where life and language had been renewed together and mated in spontaneous vigour. But in both the appeal was to mind *through* sense. In both, too, the interest was dramatic, in contrast to the reflective and descriptive modes of the eighteenth and nineteenth centuries, and to that of the subjective lyric. The Jacobeans were using the full

[5] *Poetry*. Sept. 1946.

dramatic form, but the Symbolists were dramatic in the sense in which Eliot's own early poetry is dramatic. The material is fully objectified, and does not attempt to reflect the 'personality' of the poet; and it is a poetry of ironic contrasts and oppositions, where connectives are not 'written out' in the narrative method. Instead, the figures, symbols and rhythms are held together by the tension of their inter-relationships, which again are indivisible. In the Jacobeans and Symbolists too, Eliot rediscovered the use of the full resources of language itself in poetic practice, bringing back that fusion of the simple word and the speech rhythm with all that is most rich and complex and surprising, which again had been lost to poetry for so long.

Eliot's turning to the past for his initial stimulus is an illustration of another element in his poetry which is an inseparable part of his own particular kind of symbolic transformation. There is no other poet who to the same extent, or in the same way, has used the work of other writers as an integral part of his own. He quotes with delight Ben Jonson's remark that one of the requisites of the poet, or maker, is 'Imitation, to be able to convert the substance, or riches of another poet, to his own use.' It is an aspect of the whole subject of tradition, as well as of that of the process of transformation, for Eliot's uses of allusion, adaptation and quotation serve a double purpose. They are an illustration of the possession of the 'historical sense' which 'involves a perception, not only of the pastness of the past, but of its presence; (and) compels a man to write not merely with his own generation in his bones, but with a feeling that the whole of the literature of Europe from Homer and within it the whole of the literature of his own country has a simultaneous existence and composes a simultaneous order.' [6] This rather tall order reminds us of Eliot's agreement with Matthew Arnold that the Romantic poets 'did not know enough,' and his support of Dr. Johnson's criticism of the

[6] 'Tradition and the Individual Talent,' *Selected Essays,* p. 14.

Metaphysicals that 'to write on their plan it was at least necessary to read and think.'

Even if we did not have the whole body of Eliot's criticism to prove his very wide reading, his absorption of material from it into his poetry would prove it. But it is not of course the presence of the material which is important, but the uses he makes of it. It does not only mark his sense of the continuity between past and present and between the individual writer and all other writers, but is again part of the process of the fusion of disparate materials into a recreation. The writers of earlier ages, who have become at one and the same time both past and timeless, become a fresh component in a new composition and set up new reverberations in a new context. It may be the whole spirit and outlook of other writers, who, at various periods in his development, fuse with his own consciousness and 'thence a new Concoction take.' The influences of Laforgue in his early work, of Baudelaire, Pascal, and of course most of all Dante, in his later, are illustrations of this. Or the effect may be stylistic, as with his love of Bishop Andrewes; or allusions and quotations may play the part of independent symbols, elements of the design of relationships which serve as support, or ironic contrast, or (as in 'those are pearls that were his eyes' in *The Waste Land*) as statements of theme. But they are never 'imitation' in the common sense of the word; they become revelations which are at the same time revaluations. Material from the past is amalgamated into the poem, becomes part of its 'organization' and issues in a metamorphosis.

But to see Eliot at work in actual production of the kind of poetry for which he was battling, let us take a poem first published in 1916, at a time when the public taste in England was for the 'Georgian' qualities of clear exposition, easy sentiment, and the skillful, melodious cadences of the Tennysonian tradition.

MR. APOLLINAX

Ω τῆς καινότητος. Ἡράκλεις, τῆς παραδοξολογίας,
εὐμήχανος ἄνθρωπος.

LUCIAN

When Mr. Apollinax visited the United States
His laughter tinkled among the teacups.
I thought of Fragilion, that shy figure among the
    birch-trees,
And of Priapus in the shrubbery
Gaping at the lady in the swing.
In the palace of Mrs. Phlaccus, at Professor Channing-
    Cheetah's
He laughed like an irresponsible foetus.
His laughter was submarine and profound
Like the old man of the sea's
Hidden under coral islands
Where worried bodies of drowned men drift down in
    the green silence,
Dropping from fingers of surf.
I looked for the head of Mr. Apollinax rolling under a
    chair

Or grinning over a screen
With seaweed in its hair.
I heard the beat of centaur's hoofs over the hard turf
As his dry and passionate talk devoured the afternoon.
'He is a charming man'—'But after all what did he
    mean?'—
'His pointed ears . . . He must be unbalanced,'—
'There was something he said that I might have chal-
    lenged.'
Of dowager Mrs. Phlaccus, and Professor and Mrs.
    Cheetah
I remember a slice of lemon, and a bitten macaroon.

One of the qualities for which Eliot has praised the Metaphysicals is the 'alliance of levity and seriousness' in their
poetry. It is a quality which disappeared early from his own
work, where his wit, his concentrated intellectual brilliance,

becomes steadily more serious and sardonic. But in this poem there is an agreeable mixture of grave and gay in his ironic scrutiny. The tone is set in the epigraph: [7] 'What a novelty! O Hercules, What a wonder! Man is a crafty creature of many wiles.' The main impression provoked by Mr. Apollinax is that of the complex and contradictory reactions he excites. But the poet is not concerned with explaining this effect directly. He does not deal with Mr. Apollinax as, for instance, Pope deals with Atticus, listing his attributes in an orderly sequence and coming to a savagely neat epigrammatic conclusion. But this is a satiric character sketch too, though the traits of Mr. Apollinax are not distilled into couplets which are marshalled in a logical argument of condensed satiric observation. They emerge obliquely and by implication, and in dramatic contrast to those of his environment, which is evoked too, and satirized. Moral, emotional and social criticism inhere in the symbols, but never become explicit.

Who Mr. Apollinax is does not matter. Some European man of letters, presumably, who is being lionized by the same social circle in which Mr. Prufrock and the Lady move. His name, with its hint of a synthesis of Apollo and Apollyon, suggests that mixture of the vital and the devilish which pervades his portrait. 'His laughter tinkled among the teacups' is his introduction, and it is the *vibrations* which the poet senses in the scene which are the subject matter of the poem. Those produced in Mr. Apollinax's hosts are given in the fragments of conversation at the end of the poem. They too respond to the challenge of his personality with amazement, but it is only the externals of his talk and his appearance which affect them, and they dismiss him, secure in their own unpunctured superiority and self-esteem. The poet in his turn dismisses his hosts and their environment, with laughter certainly, but the humour is wry. For the purposes of the poem, they represent the United

[7] There may be more significance than that of tone, but I have not been able to identify the passage in Lucian from which it is taken.

States, but included in the irony is all that is implied in those two words used uncapitalized to represent any wholeness of living. Their degree of inanity and inanition is suggested by the quality of their remarks, and by the details which the poet smuggles in as illustrations of the civilization they represent. The dowager entertains her academic guests in a 'palace' but the aristocracy is that of wealth only, and the names carry hints of flaccidity, pretentiousness and humbug. The scene is a tea-party, but the quality and quantity of the social, intellectual and emotional refreshment provided by the dowager and the professor and his wife is all in the poet's acid comment: 'I remember a slice of lemon and a bitten macaroon.'

Yet at the same time even the vapid observations these people make——

> 'He is a charming man'—'But after all what did he
>   mean?'
> 'His pointed ears . . . He must be unbalanced,'—

express in their own insipid way something complex and baffling about Mr. Apollinax which the poet feels too and for which *he* must find the *appropriate* verbal medium. That medium must be a sensuous embodiment of the material, so the laughter and talk of Mr. Apollinax—and he is defined purely in terms of his laughter and talk—is communicated to us entirely through their impact on the *senses;* by the pictures we see, the sounds we hear, the associations they arouse, and the rhythms through which they reach us.

What has registered to one of the ladies as his pointed ears, has already affected the poet, listening to his tinkling laughter, as a memory of the delicate but lascivious flavor of a picture in the manner of Fragonard's *The Swing*. The addition of Priapus, the lewd garden god, 'gaping' in the shrubbery, emphasizes the sexual element felt strongly in Mr. Apollinax, but that element has been subdued to a stylized convention. In the present setting however his laughter takes on a different quality:

> In the palace of Mrs. Phlaccus, at Professor Channing-
> Cheetah's
> He laughed like an irresponsible foetus.

The impudent rhyme brings the desiccated, flaccid, utra-respectable society figures into sharp collision with something utterly different in quality, though as inhuman in its way as its opposite. The ironic laughter is timeless and bodiless and all pervasive, existing before birth and after death. It is a detached and irrepressible vital force, and in one way it is refreshing and surprising to feel it, 'unbalanced'—rolling around and peering over the screen these inhibited and hidebound figures put between themselves and reality.

> I looked for the head of Mr. Apollinax rolling under
> a chair
> Or grinning over a screen
> With seaweed in its hair.

But the laughter also has an element of irresponsibility and insensitivity. Mr. Apollinax's hosts are also insensitive in their way. They lack entirely what Henry James describes as 'the tendency of the artist to vibrate'; they are flat, dull, doughy in their self-complacent egotism. But the egotism betrayed by Mr. Apollinax's laughter and talk, while again it is very compelling in its sheer primitive power, has something horrible in its all-devouring assertiveness. His laughter is 'submarine and profound,' but it suggests the incarnation of the ocean into that sinister mythical figure, the old man of the sea, and there is no 'levity' in the lines where Eliot pictures him laughing,

> Hidden under coral islands
> Where worried bodies of drowned men drift down in
> the green silence,
> Dropping from fingers of surf.

The 'worried' here carries its etymological origin of *strangled* or *torn*. Suddenly the hands holding the teacup and the maca-roon turn into the fingers of surf and the clutches of the old man of the sea; and though we are back again in a moment in the tone of light mockery, the 'vibration' has been felt.

The same hint of something repellent in its insensitive drive is in the description of his talk. There the common cliché of 'riding roughshod' over others, and suggested in the Professor's belated regret: 'There was something he said I might have challenged,' becomes:

> I heard the beat of centaur's hoofs over the hard turf
> As his dry and passionate talk devoured the afternoon.

This evokes a wonderful contrast between academic timidity and conventional torpor and the swift racing vitality of the centaur. It also illustrates the blending and condensing of suggestions in a single image, of which Eliot is such a master. Mr. Apollinax eating his tea and appropriating all the conversation; the sound of his voice; and the quality of his personality which comes through the talk. It is full of vitality, but again it is an assertive, unrefreshing, greedy vitality which the image creates.

The poem thus translates into images and sensations everything the poet wants to convey about the actual scene and all the vibrations it sets up in the way of emotional and intellectual responses. But it is much more than mere brilliant impressionistic notation. It has a complex structure of interweaving dramatic oppositions running all through its deceptively erratic course. The stuffy Cambridge drawing-room is seen in turn against the atmosphere of a sylvan eighteenth century painting; against an emblem of the life-principle; against a mythological embodiment of the destructive forces of the ocean, and another of the blended vigour of man and beast. But another contrast is that between the sensibility of the poet, as illustrated in his rich field of associations, and the savourless prosaic remarks of his hosts; and yet another is in the conflicting aspects of Mr. Apollinax himself. Finally the darting, diverse nature of the whole experience is emphasized not only by the quality of the images themselves, but by the irregular metre and rhyme scheme, and by the intermingling of the general light conversational tone with the sad lingering music of the lines telling of the drowned men, and the swift energy of those evoking the dominating beat of the centaur's hoofs.

The poem is something in the nature of an exercise in technique, and it is a good illustration of the disciplines which Eliot had been practicing in secret and which were to be the bases of all his later development: the union of idea, emotion and sensation in the symbol and image; the mastery of rhythmic variation; the dramatic structure of antithesis; the expansion of the surface of the occasion into a symbolic pattern of wider issues; and the economy and concentration with which that pattern is projected.

In the preface to the 1928 edition of *The Sacred Wood*, Eliot says that the problem which is central to the essays is that of 'the integrity of poetry'—poetry considered primarily as poetic art and not as anything else. The cause for which he was battling in 1920 was that assertion; that poetry is not 'self-expression,' but the making of a new integration which is independent of the life of the poet. That was where the emphasis of his criticism then fell. In the eight years that had passed since the first publication he found that his emphasis had shifted, and that something had happened to his mind which was 'not so much a change or reversal of opinion, as an expansion and development of interests.' He had passed on to another critical problem, 'that of the relation of poetry to the spiritual and social life of its time and of other times.' A great part of any criticism of Eliot's own poetry is necessarily taken up with these later interests, but it is right to emphasize at the start that it is his techniques as an artist which are the means through which the ends in social and spiritual revelation are attained. The conclusion of the poetry is an illumination of life, but it is the principles and practice of the artist which are, as he says, 'logically, as well as chronologically, the beginning.'

CHAPTER III

Early Poems 1909-1920

All creativeness in the realm of the spirit . . . arises
from a state of mental suffering, and it is spiritual stagnation, psychic sterility, which causes this state.

C. JUNG. *Psychotherapists or the Clergy?*

IN HIS essay on Dante, Eliot confesses that he found it
difficult at first to accept the end of the *Purgatorio* and
the whole of the *Paradiso* because of a prejudice 'that
poetry not only must be found *through* suffering but can find
its materials only *in* suffering.' Elsewhere he speaks of 'the
struggle—which alone constitutes life for the poet—to transmute his personal and private agonies into something rich and
strange, something universal and impersonal.' He does not
mention that the poet's personal and private joys can be treated
in the same way, and indeed in the whole of Eliot's poetry
suffering plays a very much larger part than joy. Hell and
purgatory are familiar territories to him; release from them
fleeting and infrequent, won only by unrelenting self-discipline,
'a *training* of the soul as severe and ascetic as the training of
the body of a runner'; the comfort in the pain only that 'the
souls in purgatory suffer because they *wish to suffer,* for
purgation.' The main distinction in most of his poetry is not
between suffering and joy but between two kinds of suffering:
the passive and the active. He sees the choice for civilized man
as between the pain of spiritual stagnation and psychic sterility
or the pain of the willing surrender to purgation, to the heavy
toil of spiritual rebirth and growth.

The early poems show us 'the immense panorama of futility

and anarchy which is contemporary history,' and the condition of the poet as a part of it. For he differs from others in the same environment only in his awareness of his plight. From these poems it is clear that it was not only the technical disciplines of the Jacobean dramatists and of the French Symbolists which attracted Eliot to those poets. He shares too their spiritual colouring; an attitude of disgust at the quality of the civilization in which they find themselves, and an added self-disgust. There is a sense of imprisonment in an empty, ugly and alien society, and the impossibility of escape from it. The poet can do nothing but escape into his poetry. There he can examine his situation, objectify and dramatize it. He can create in patterned language the moods of ironic and cynical repulsion, of unromantic disillusionment and of nervous intensity which mirror his predicament. He can transmute its welter of triviality and horror into a wealth of related symbolic detail.

There are two backgrounds in the earliest poems—those contained in *Prufrock and Other Observations* (1917); the social environment of the poet's own class, and the plebeian. In some we are in the drawing-rooms of a society 'refined beyond the point of civilization,' among the teacups and the cakes and the coffee spoons, or tête-à-tête with a lady in a setting of flowers or candle-light, with the conversation slipping 'among velleities and carefully caught regrets,' and embarrassing overtures towards intimacy. We have glimpses of the solid older generation reading *The Boston Evening Transcript,* and living and dying imperturbed among their servants and dogs and parrots, and of the younger generation at home or abroad, being 'modern' and sophisticated. At the other extreme there is the impact on the senses of all the ugliness and squalor of the common urban scene; the sight of the 'broken blinds and chimney pots,' of vacant lots with their grimy scraps of newspaper, of sunless dry geraniums, of hands raising dingy shades in furnished rooms; the sounds of rattling plates in basement kitchens, of sparrows in the gutters, of insistent feet pressing the sawdust-trampled street. Above all there are the smells; of steak in passageways, of stale beer, of cocktails and ciga- rettes, of dusty paper flowers, of females in shuttered rooms.

But it is apparent at once that the outward scene never exists for its own sake, that the world which is being created from these sensory impressions and concrete objects is a world of emotional realities. The outward scene exists as a set of symbols, 'a thousand sordid images,' through which the imag- ination senses the quality of a civilization not of an environ- ment. The music, 'dying with a dying fall' in the drawing- rooms, is no longer the food of love, but of death. That evening which is 'spread out against the sky/Like a patient etherised upon a table,' is no placid, peaceful city sunset. It fills the imagination with thoughts of disease and helplessness; of the ether which is not the breath of the spirit, but the deadener of consciousness and volition; of the contrast between the wide stretches of the sky and the vigour and vitality of man reduced to the living death of anaesthesia. 'The burnt-out ends of smoky days' are not the city dusk but the twilight of an epoch; 'the yellow fog that rubs its back upon the window panes,' the dinginess, the stale smells, are the creeping, choking atmos- phere of a spiritual miasma; the 'crowd of twisted things,' the 'broken spring in the factory yard,/Rust that clings to the form that the strength has left' are emblems of moral, not material disintegration; the 'one-night cheap hotels' are not a reminder of the transient life of a great city, but of the home- lessness of the human soul.

And so with the figures which move about in this world. It is their states of mind and not their social status which matters: attitudes not actualities. Brahmin or plebeian backgrounds make no difference; a common blight afflicts them both, a com- mon impoverishment of vitality, a common lack of meaning. These people either live by the 'formulated phrases' of social and religious faiths which are unreal and devitalized, dry and sapless as a 'twisted branch upon the beach'; or their lives are

purely materialistic; or they are conscious to a lesser or greater
degree of their isolation and rootlessness, their insecurity and
sterility. The 'lonely men in shirtsleeves leaning out of win-
dows,' the 'damp souls of housemaids, sprouting despondently
at area gates,' 'the aimless smiles of the passersby,' are all
expressions of the negative helplessness enveloping this world.
Those more conscious or more sensitive are the victims of a
more positive torment. They agonize, like Mr. Prufrock, over
their own vacillations, timidities and frustrations; or lie sleep-
less, with souls 'stretched tight across the sky . . . Or tram-
pled by insistent feet'; or feel 'the last twist of the knife' in
the realization that the dreary routine of living is as much a
nightmare as the distortions and disintegrations of 'a lunar
synthesis' in which 'the floors of memory' have been dissolved.

The Love Song of J. Alfred Prufrock, written in 1910-11,
is the richest of these poems, and illustrates very fully the insights which are particularly characteristic of Eliot's new vision
and the disciplines through which he presented it. Mr. Prufrock
is at the opposite extreme from Mr. Apollinax as a 'personality pattern.' He would indeed be helplessly envious of Mr.
Apollinax's uninhibited self-assertion as he 'devoured the afternoon,' and of his unrestrained vitality as he 'laughed like
an irresponsible foetus.' For Mr. Prufrock is an unromantic
and unprincely Hamlet in a 'tragical-comical-historical' urban
drama where 'Denmark's a prison'—the prison of a divided
self in the tortures of neurotic conflict. His 'love song,' as the
epigraph implies, will never be uttered outside the inferno of
his own mind, and the 'you and I' of his soliloquy are the
impulses within him 'to murder and create' or 'to be or not
to be,' concluding neither in suicide nor in the release of chosen
action, but in the death-in-life of the abdication of the will.

As in *Mr. Apollinax,* the method of presentation is that of
dramatic opposition, but here it is expanded and subtleized
and demands more literary background and imaginative agility

on the part of the reader. The social environment in which
Mr. Prufrock is 'drowned' is as inane and stifling and self-
satisfied as that which Mr. Apollinax dominates so easily, and
it is evoked with the same brilliant sensuous embodiment in
image, word and rhythm. But it is the 'universe' of Mr. Prufrock himself which is the centre of interest. And in creating
that, Eliot is already expanding the possibilities of the 'mythical method' as a way of ordering and controlling his material.
Mr. Prufrock's retreat into the world of despairing introspec-
tive day-dream, and his mingled self-pity and self-disgust,
are not only brought home to us through the images of the
tortuous streets and the fog-cat, the pictures of his life as
measured out with coffee spoons, and the symbols of his
terror of social and sexual failure. The shrunken universe of
his own nature and will is set beside a series of suggestions
and allusions which take us to worlds of action and expression
which are very different. John the Baptist, Lazarus, Hesiod's
Works and Days, Michelangelo and Shakespeare all 'disturb'
Mr. Prufrock's pitifully enclosed universe. Most of all, the
sustained parallel with the concepts of time and space and
love in Marvell's *To His Coy Mistress* provides a melody
in counterpoint to his own 'dying fall.' They haunt his own
dickerings with *his* 'world' and 'time,' and mock ironically his
own impotence to 'force the moment to its crisis.'

Finally his psychological plight reveals itself in the identification of both the positive and negative elements of his
conflict with images of the sea, primordial symbol of both
creation and destruction. At the end of the poem, he hears
the mermaids singing and has a vision of them

> riding seaward on the waves
> Combing the white hair of the waves blown back
> When the wind blows the water white and black.

That glimpse of a life-rhythm where living creatures delight
spontaneously in their natural environment, mastering it and

being carried along with its vital energies, is what Mr. Prufrock's 'I' yearns for and will never achieve. All that his 'we' has done is to capitulate:

> We have lingered in the chambers of the sea
> By sea-girls wreathed with seaweed red and brown
> Till human voices wake us, and we drown.

He has withdrawn into passive day-dream, where the 'arms that are braceleted and white and bare' caress and crown him as he lies catlike 'smoothed by long fingers' in a peaceful sleep. The inevitable future awakening will be only to suffocate in the human scene, again a part of the living death of the patient on the operating table.

His outburst in the middle of the poem where he accepts the hopelessness of struggle suggests the same compulsive infantile and primitive craving:

> I should have been a pair of ragged claws
> Scuttling across the floors of silent seas.

Here on one level, the claws suggest the longing for uncomplicated animal existence. They can clutch their prey and make off with it, without any preface of 'Do I dare?' or 'Shall I say?' They, like the mermaids, are at home and free in the 'silent seas' and can scuttle as they desire. But at the same time, they cannot go *forward*. As Hamlet says to Polonius: 'Yourself, sir, shall grow old as I am, if like a crab you could go backward.' Mr. Prufrock laments 'I grow old . . . I grow old . . . ,' but like Hamlet, his secret wish is only to regress to a safe haven where his inner universe is no longer disturbed by any tormenting human problems.

In the next volume of poems, published three years later, while the suffering presented is still that of spiritual stagnation and psychic sterility against the background of a world steeped in the same atmosphere, the poetry itself has taken on an enriched vigour and expansion. The method by which a definite parallel is manipulated between the planless panorama of the present and the ordered world of myth, appears for the first time. Whereas in the earlier volume *Prufrock* is the only poem in which a conflict between contemporary isolation, disintegration and sterility and the awareness of an existing and unused power is even hinted at, all the finest poems in the 1920 volume are concerned with the dramatic opposition of the world of today to the sources of vitality and order from which it is now cut off and of which it has the most urgent need. The rival forces are not yet engaged in the poet's own consciousness; he is involved in no personal struggle between them. He *perceives*, and recreates his perceptions by projecting patterns which are now much more than those of the nerves upon a screen. The insights are increasingly moral as well as emotional, they are coloured by a disgust which is much more bitter and searching, and the powerful symbols and rhythms which carry them move in new and complex poetic pantomime and choreography.

Some of the juxtapositions are comparatively simple: the more or less innocent materialism of the secular world, compared with the hypocritical materialism of the 'True Church' in *The Hippopotamus;* the romantic and classical symbols of lustful passions beside the sordid scene in the rooming house of *Sweeney Erect;* the childish day-dreams of dazzling successes compared with the actuality of the stale and unsavoury emotional present in *A Cooking Egg.* The present, indeed is uniformly stale and unsavoury in all these poems, as it is in the earlier ones, but interwoven with it is the continuous reminder of times when it was not so, and of works of the creative imagination in art and thought which have embodied a different reality and pictured a different vision. And the dramatic interplay and organization of these antagonisms becomes increasingly intricate and concentrated in its suggestions.

Sometimes indeed, too much so, as in *Mr. Eliot's Sunday*

Morning Service, where by the time the reader has finished
with the Encyclopedia Britannica and the Oxford English
Dictionary he has not much heart for the intellectual *tour-de-
force* of the use of the material in the poem. Like *The Hippopotamus* it is a satire on the decay of religion, but a very much
more complex one. On the one side, or in the centre rather,
there is the basic Christian concept, 'In the beginning was the
Word,' twice stated; also two verses describing an Italian
painting:

> A painter of the Umbrian school
> Designed upon a gesso ground
> The nimbus of the Baptized God.
> The wilderness is cracked and browned
>
> But through the water pale and thin
> Still shine the unoffending feet
> And there above the painter set
> The Father and the Paraclete.

The lines are full of implications; of the creative mystery of
the Logos; of the rich symbolic content of the sacrament of
baptism and the doctrine of the Trinity; of the simple humanity of the still-shining figure, still reminding man in the modern
'wilderness' of the redemption of his 'offences'; and of the
whole 'design' which the painter has 'set' on his ground. In
ironic contrast Eliot sets various symbols of degradation and
ugliness and a complicated parallel between the sterility of the
worker-bees and that of the 'Word' of sectarian theological
argument. The 'superfetation of τὸ ἕν,' that is, the effort to
fertilize 'the one' by a fresh begetting; to make of the Word a
Queen bee mated with numerous drones, inevitably produces a
swarm of neuter religions, symbolized by the heretical Origen,
the self-made eunuch. The sterile 'masters of the subtle schools'
who think themselves 'sapient sutlers of the Lord' (servers or
food-bringers) are barren. Not only as barren as the bees, but
as barren in meaning to common humanity as the appalling

polysyllables and learned terms with which the poem is loaded. The only area in it where this 'neuter' use of the 'word' is not used is in the two verses describing the painting.

The neuter worker-bees, also 'sapient sutlers,' at least fertilize the flowers as their 'hairy bellies' gather the pollen, and so may be said to perform a 'blest office' in the scheme of nature; but the same cannot be said of the 'blest office' of the church service, or of 'the sapient sutlers of the Lord' who are the clergy and congregation. The 'sable presbyters' move up the aisle like the 'religious caterpillars' in the epigraph, who were more interested in getting the Jew of Malta's 'piaculative pence' than in saving his soul. The black gowns and red, spotty faces and the 'dim souls' of the devout congregation all contrast with the shining halo and the pale thin water and 'unoffending feet.'

The final degrading 'offence' is the contrast of Sweeney wallowing in his bath with the figure of the Baptized God; with the further irony that there is a parallel between the movement of his body, shifting from ham to ham and stirring the water, and the 'controversial' antics of the learned theologians.

There is as much packed symbolism and verbal concentration in *Burbank with a Baedaker: Bleistein with a Cigar,* but the materials are much more lively and the versification more agile and flexible in its phrasing. The epigraph strings together and telescopes quotations from writers (St. Augustine, Henry James, Shakespeare, Browning) whose life or work associates itself with Venice or with thoughts aroused in the poet by the contemplation of Venice today. The poem itself, by selecting, combining and contrasting details in a pattern of interweaving oppositions, makes a design where again it is the sterility, ugliness and decadence of 'contemporaneity' which stand out. The details are a medley of direct sense impressions and of references which evoke specific works of art and their aura of association.

It opens deceptively as if it were going to employ the 'narrative method':

> Burbank crossed a little bridge
>   Descending at a small hotel;
> Princess Volupine arrived,
>   They were together, and he fell.

But the next verse alters the focus from a temporal to a spatial one.

> Defunctive music under sea
>   Passed seaward with the passing bell
> Slowly: the God Hercules
>   Had left him, that had loved him well.

This remains obscure unless we remember the scene in *Anthony and Cleopatra,* before the battle of Actium, where the soldiers hear strange unearthly music and one of them declares:

> 'Tis the god Hercules, whom Antony lov'd
> Now leaves him.

From then on it is clear that Burbank, the Princess, Bleistein and Sir Ferdinand Klein are not actors in a realistic drama, but are symbolic embodiments in a conflict of values. Burbank with his Baedeker, embodiment of creative arts and acts, becomes aware of his impotence in the Venice of today. Associated with the 'small' and 'little,' he descends and falls in the first verse; the 'passing bell' of his music is 'defunctive' in the second. His virility has left him; and in the last verse he contemplates the proud winged lion on its pillar by the waterfront, epitomizing the power and glory of the old city, and asks:

> Who clipped the lion's wings
> And flea'd his rump and pared his claws?

This actualization into direct physical terms of diminution

and decay colours the whole poem. The loss of the long tradition
in Venice of aristocracy built on commercial wealth mating
with culture through the patronage of artists, is part of 'time's
ruins.' The Princess, whose name suggests at once the foxy
and the sensual, the decayed aristocrat fallen to adventuress,
and in physical terms 'in a decline,' 'extends' not patronage to
the arts, but 'a meagre, blue-nailed phthisic hand,' to the new
commercial order, symbolized by Sir Ferdinand Klein. Again,
the quality of that new order emerges in contrasted terms of
form and energy between Bleistein and his surroundings in the
poem. His 'saggy bending of the knees/And elbows, with the
palms turned out' is first set beside the great bronze horses
over the doors of St. Mark's, as their hooves 'beat up the dawn'
as if harnessed to the chariot of Apollo. Then the reference
to 'Her shuttered barge/ Burned on the water all the day'
injects the memory of Tiepolo's great frescoes of Antony and
Cleopatra in the Palazzio Labia. Finally, as we read

> A lustreless protrusive eye
> Stares from the protozoic slime
> At a perspective of Canaletto

his 'saggy bending' contrasts with the formal perfection of the
picture. At the same time his 'lustreless' eye contrasts with
Canaletto's lighting, and backwards, with the light of the dawn
over the lagoon, and the memory of Cleopatra's barge as it
'burned on the water all the day.' Istria, Antony and Cleopatra,
Canaletto 'decline' into 'the smoky candle end of time,' or the
'lights' by which the Princess entertains her new patron. In
further cross-fertilizations of the images, the standards and
stability of the past are suggested by the association of the
'perspective,' 'the seven laws,' and the quotation 'On the Rialto
once.' This last brings not only the memory of the bridge
itself, but the whole world of *The Merchant of Venice*. 'The
rats are underneath the piles'—the foundations of that world,

built on its attitude towards usury. They have become 'saggy'
by the new commercialism, symbolized here, as in *Gerontion*,
as 'the jew.'

Thus with the utmost concentration and economy of language, but with the widest possible expansion of it by
suggestion and association, Eliot contrives to manipulate this
'continuous parallel between contemporaneity and antiquity.'
All the music of the past is 'defunctive'; all its ordered civilization dying into a new barbarism; all its light and glory gutter-
ing to extinction.

In *Burbank* the opposition is a clear-cut one between the
values of the past and of the present, but in *Sweeney among
the Nightingales* the emphasis is rather upon the distinction
between two atmospheres, two attitudes towards reality. On
the one hand there is human life conceived in a religious and
moral framework, surrounded by spiritual forces and by
natural forces of which it is a living part; on the other, there
is the disintegrated, rootless, unstable, isolated position of the
individual in the midst of the futility and anarchy of pure
materialism. There is, of course, no overt reference to this.
After the setting of the first two verses the drama sweeps in
one long sentence of descriptive vision to the climax which
links Agamemnon with the contemporary scene. That, and the
epigraph from Aeschylus, 'Alas, I have been smitten deep with
a mortal blow,' lead some readers to seek a parallel in the
action between the murder of Agamemnon and the scene in the
poem. But it seems more characteristic of Eliot that the relationships should be symbolic; that it is everything that Agamemnon and his story (and myth in general) stands for, that
has been killed by Sweeney and his like.

The link between the two worlds, that of myth and of the
immediate actuality, is the nightingales. They are present in
both, but Sweeney and his companions do not hear them. They

are as deaf to their song as to the story behind the song. It is a horrible story of cruelty and revenge, just as the Agamemnon myth is, and the story of the 'bloody wood.' Here Eliot is using a favorite device of his, the telescoping of associations to get greater pressure and intensity. Agamemnon, after all, was not killed in a wood. The wood is that from which Frazer named his great work *The Golden Bough,* and from which Eliot took the title for his first essays, *The Sacred Wood,* where he uses it as a symbol for the immortal poetic tradition, always dying and being reborn. The opening chapter of Frazer traces the story of the wood of Nemi, which was the scene of the bloody ritual by which the old priest of the grove was slain by a younger one, who succeeded as both priest and king until he in his turn was slain. Frazer shows how this ritual is the basis for all the oldest symbols of the human race. It was bound up with the concept of the Fertility God and his resurrection every spring, and extended into the larger theme of the death and resurrection of the human spirit. Eliot's purpose is to emphasize that pattern. Philomela is raped, but magical powers render her voice inviolable and immortal. It lives on in a bird, linking together man and nature, the animal and the spiritual. Agamemnon is murdered and Clytemnestra is murdered and Orestes is pursued by the Furies, but the end of the trilogy is the transcendence of revenge by reconciliation and mercy— just as the Sacred Heart too embodies the same values. All these stories create a pattern of reality which gives *meaning* to human hate and horror and sacrifice and suffering, because they are related to an order and value beyond the temporal and immediate. Agamemnon too represents another tradition, that of the heroic ideal of Greek tragedy. He is king and leader; his fate involves the whole community and its laws, and the irony of fate, and the inexorable working out of the tragic pattern.

The basic ironic contrasts of the poem are those between the suggestions of the significance of life seen in such terms of

value and order and the complete *in*significance of the modern
scene. These people have not even the vitality to have violent
passions of any sort. Their 'murderous paws' tear only grapes;
their sexual passion is that of a drunken prostitute trying to sit
on Sweeney's knees; the outcome of the assault is only to pull
off a tablecloth and overturn a coffee-cup. They move in the
clearest pictorial outline, vividly *there* by the selection of a few
expressive details, but there is no point at which they have any
organic relationship with the worlds of spiritual value, of
nature, or of human fellowship; no point at which they touch
the patterns suggested by the worlds of classical myth, of
heroic tragedy, or of the Convent. They are indeed barely
human. They are largely designated in animal terms, and thus
dehumanized, and as men and women they have neither identity nor community. They do not even speak. Sweeney himself
is simply a laugh, in a body which otherwise suggests an ape,
a zebra or a giraffe; one woman is 'the person in the Spanish
cape,' the other is Rachel—she was born with another name
but she does not use it any more. The second man is 'the silent
vertebrate in brown,' and his reaction as he 'contracts and concentrates' suggests a lower form of life than a vertebrate, that
of an amoeba seen under a microscope. The third man is heavy
and lifeless, the only gleam about him is that of the gold fillings
in his teeth. And they are not even finely co-ordinated animals.
Again, in terms of gesture, Eliot suggests the disintegrated
quality of life they symbolize. They *sprawl,* they *gape,* they
'show fatigue.' The woman *slips* in her tipsy efforts to seduce
Sweeney: even her 'reorganisation' upon the floor is only to
yawn and pull up a stocking, and is an ironic comment on the
concept of organisation.

These people have neither vitality nor order, and Eliot places
them against a background which has both. The punctuation is
significant here. After the introduction of Sweeney as a medley
of animal shapes and markings, there are six lines of complete
contrast which put him within a cosmic setting. There is no

period at the end of these lines, just a semi-colon, and the sentence runs on to the end of the poem and the final climax of the Convent, the nightingales, the bloody wood and Agamemnon. The contemporary scene, that is, fades in from the background of the great ordered rhythms of the natural world, and fades out into the reminders of the great ordered patterns of myth. The worlds of the temporal and the eternal are always co-existent. The permanence of the rhythmic patterns of nature, the moon and stars, the seas and the rivers are still there, just as the deathless reality of Agamemnon, and the bloody wood and the nightingales and the Sacred Heart are still there. But their clarity and brightness is lost and their relationship with humanity. The stormy moon is blurred; it 'slides' to its setting towards the shallowest of rivers, with the ominous 'drift' of doom about it. All the myths linking man and the heavens and the gods and so drawing them all into one pattern, are 'veiled'; the sea itself, symbol of life, is 'hushed' and 'shrunken'; the true dreams which come through the gates of horn in the underworld are blocked by the figure of Sweeney.

Just as these people can establish no contact with the old cosmic visions, the scene without, so the scene within is equally 'shrunken.' That suggestion is built up from many details in the few verses of description. Of course there are sexual overtones in the fruits, just as there are to the actions of the man in brown, but in the general context the point is that the fruits they eat are all foreign fruits. They do not plant them or raise them or share in any way in the natural rhythms of growth and fruition. It is the same with the cultures and nationalities to which they have belonged. The traditions of Ireland or Russia, of Catholicism or Judaism mean nothing in their lives. Nor does the mere bond of a common humanity unite them. Everyone is distrustful and wary; if two are 'in league' it is for some sordid purpose; an advance towards a relationship is only a 'gambit,' a move in a game to beat the other fellow; the host converses 'apart.' Everything indeed is 'apart'; there is no community, no cohesion; all is blurred, indistinct, disordered, fragmentary. There is no framework which circumscribes it and within which it has composition and meaning. The only symbols with meaning are *outside,* where the sky and the woods and the Convent are all framed by the branches of wistaria. But that view is effectively blocked by the man with the 'heavy eyes,' and all the expansion into dignity and tradition brought in by the word *circumscribe* is at once cancelled by its conjunction with his golden grin. Just as Sweeney blocks the horned gate, so that the messages from the shades—the human tradition—cannot get through, so the vertebrate in brown blocks the window on to the immediate realities. But the point is that outside in the dim night *are* the Convent and the nightingales and the wood and the memory of the dead Agamemnon, and all the associations they bring, about the relationships of man and nature and the gods, of mortality and immortality, death and resurrection, the temporal and the eternal, nature and spirit. Man is animal, inescapably so; and in a sense every shroud is a stained and dishonoured one; all are 'maculate.' But the nightingale is not only animal, nor the Agamemnon story one only of dishonour. Their perspective is in a larger context.

CHAPTER IV

◆◆◆

Gerontion

> He could not escape suffering and he could not transcend it . . . But what he could do . . . was to study his suffering.
>
> T. S. ELIOT. *Baudelaire*

THERE is only one poem of any length in the 1920 volume, but it is one of Eliot's most powerful, and one of his most obscure. It is impossible to read it without being deeply stirred by its strange drama and music, but to interpret the sequence of its imaginative logic is not easy, and there has to be a good deal of guesswork. The organization, however, is similar to that of *Sweeney among the Nightingales* in that there is the same antithesis between human life conceived in a framework of myth and the lack of all meaning in contemporary secularism. In *Gerontion*, the general context of myth becomes specifically that of Christianity. The birth of Christ is conceived of as opening a new era, within which the cycle of civilization symbolized by Gerontion is very near its end. Gerontion sees one aspect of Christ as the tiger, Blake's embodiment of the creative fire and light in animal form, part of the order of nature, but he is as incapable of drawing any vitality from, or entering into any communion with, that elemental source of 'juvescence' as was Mr. Prufrock from the sea and its mermaids. Like Mr. Prufrock, he lays bare his psychological dilemma with merciless ironic insight, but at the same time excuses himself from translating self-knowledge into any effort towards change. Indeed, like Mr. Prufrock, he feels above all the futility of struggle. All his acute activity of consciousness is in *perception*, and is not directed towards any solution. He

47

supplies admirable reasons, indeed, for the impossibility of any solution. But his perceptions are far wider and deeper and more intense than those of Mr. Prufrock, and they operate in a different theatre. Instead of a setting within a recognizable environment, which keeps the mind busy with precise social implications, the whole vision is distanced, suspended out of time, projected from 'a dull head among windy spaces' and forming itself into pictures and psychic situations with a dream locus and ambience of their own.

The epigraph takes us to *Measure for Measure,* to the Duke's speech when he visits Claudio, under sentence of death in prison. He urges him to wish for death, to 'be absolute for death,' and to reason on the lines that what is called life is little but conflict, cowardice, insecurity, disease and the scramble for riches. The inevitable end is 'palsied eld' which has 'neither heat, affection, limb nor beauty.'

> What's yet in this
> That bears the name of life?

he asks, and in the poem, Eliot creates life seen in those terms as the civilization in which Gerontion exists. It is a civilization founded on money values and secular rationalism, with no religious communion or human sense of community, a nightmare world of isolation and instability, of restless nervous and intellectual activity, emotional stagnation and spiritual drought. Gerontion (the name means a little old man) is the shadowy symbol and spokesman of the sensitive intellectual in this world. Perhaps we are meant to compare him with the hero of Newman's *The Dream of Gerontius,* who looks forward with such full and serene joy and faith to the moment of dissolution and the acceptance of purgation. The diminutive of the name would imply the diminution of the life in Eliot's hero. He has become contracted to nothing but 'a dull head': 'I have lost my passion . . . I have lost my sight, smell, hearing, taste and touch,' he says, and 'I have no ghosts.'

But that does not apply to his creator. The truth of Gerontion's situation is 'carried alive into the heart by passion'; it is felt in every line in terms of sensation; and the poet's imagination is filled with 'ghosts,' with suggestions and associations and memories which charge his strange imagery and powerful rhythms. The negative deprivation of Gerontion and his dream world, possessing 'neither heat, affection, limb nor beauty,' is revealed in most telling detail by its physical characteristics. The whole vision is 'thoughts of a dry brain in a dry season'; Gerontion has been driven by the parching trade winds, steadily blowing in the same direction, into 'a sleepy corner'; his house is peeling and decayed, and he 'stiffens' in it, passive and inert, 'waiting for rain,' surrounded both within and without by emblems of degradation. A boy reads to him from a history of the past, and as he listens, his thoughts flow into an imaginative 'inquisition' of his own situation and that of the other 'tenants of the house' who share his arid and humiliating exile and whom he is addressing. Momentarily he is swept out of his inertia into gusts of dramatic challenge, and the need of self-examination, self-explanation and self-justification. His apologia moves back and forth from historical revelation to cynical or impassioned analysis to embittered disgust to declamatory warning. From reverie it passes to direct rhetorical approach: 'Think now . . . think now . . .,' and with a tormented desire to convince himself and his hearers of what is plainly untrue, he proclaims:

> Think at last
> We have not reached conclusions, when I
> Stiffen in a rented house. Think at last
> I have not made this show purposely . . .

With an effort at calm objectivity he goes on 'I would meet you upon this honestly,' but it is immediately apparent that his only purpose is an attempt at self-vindication from his self-brought charge, and that he himself knows that his 'conclusion' is already irrevocable.

A sequence of visual images and physical details in the opening paragraph reveals his condition and the reasons for it. He points at once to the chief element in his failure: he has not *fought*. In 1920, when the poem was published, the first World War was but barely over, but that had been no Thermopylae, no active struggle of the forces of civilization against barbarism, refreshed, in spite of hardships, by the 'warm rain' of faith in a common cause. Nor has Gerontion throughout his life fought for any values he believes in. His inert helpless old age is the result of a passive comfort-seeking indolence. But it has not brought him any comfort, and the description of his 'house' and his debased and impoverished living conditions follow. The civilization he represents is decayed:

> And the jew squats on the window sill, the owner,
> Spawned in some estaminet of Antwerp,
> Blistered in Brussels, patched and peeled in London.

As a result of not fighting for the values of a living tradition, the modern world is now 'owned' and enslaved by the only proliferating element in it, the international money power. The inhuman and sub-human quality of that power is suggested in the words *squats* and *spawned*. Then the landlord and the house, the owner and the civilization he owns, become one. They share the degradation and they share the syntax, and are both 'blistered, patched and peeled' in their shabby and rotting decay. The background to the 'house' is a field of 'rocks, moss, stonecrop, iron, merds'—an atmosphere of barrenness, torpor, mechanization and corruption, where even natural lust itself, the goat, is starved and unhealthy. The picture is completed by the figure of the woman. She is equally squalid. Instead of functioning as mother and helpmate, symbol of fertility and affections, she is the petty housekeeper with petty ailments. In another compression of the syntax we see her 'poking the

peevish gutter.' Finally Gerontion sums *himself* up as 'a dull
head among windy spaces.' He is not a whole man, symbolic
of a civilization ministering to body, mind and spirit. He has
shrunk to an abstract intelligence, anchored to nothing stable,
with no organic relationship between himself and a living
culture.

In an abrupt, startling transition we pass from this symbolic
description to obscure condensed intensity of suggestion. Eliot
has said that if many images highly charged with emotional
significance are fused together, intensity is gained at the expense of clarity, and these next few lines illustrate this. Yet
they are the heart of the poem. With the demand of the Phari-
sees to Christ: 'We would see a sign,' we are shown the direction of the thought. The sign was given, but the modern world
has taken the revelation with doubt and questioning. Bishop
Andrewes, in a Nativity sermon, described the mystery of the
Word made flesh appearing first as a speechless infant, as 'the
word within a word unable to speak a word.' Eliot adds the
words 'swaddled with darkness.' That mystery of the union of
flesh and *logos* remains dumb and hidden, its spiritual meaning
unable to make itself known.

> In the juvescence of the year
> Came Christ the tiger
>
> In depraved May, dogwood and chestnut, flowering
>   judas,
> To be eaten, to be divided, to be drunk
> Among whispers;

I interpret this that just as the significance of the symbol of
Incarnation has been ignored, so has the symbolism of Blake's
The Tyger. He saw the tiger as the symbol of the union of the
creator and his creation; the symbol of the energy of the cre-

ator expressing itself in all forms of physical incarnation. Eliot suggests the link between the human and the natural world in associating the *year,* the seasonal cycle of birth and death, with juvescence, the youthfulness of a human being. The tiger also of course suggests the 'burning bright in the forests of the night' compared with the 'swaddled with darkness.' But it is in quite a different forest that this tiger appears. The next lines are very obscure. At one level they might mean that Christ as tiger superseded the old pagan sexual Fertility rituals and myths of 'dismemberment,' giving them new sacramental meaning. But I follow Ruth Bailey [1] in believing that the break in the verse paragraph here indicates a gap in time, and that 'depraved May, dogwood and chestnut, flowering judas,' besides pointing back to the old paganism, points forward to the birth of a new paganism, and opposes the Renaissance to the Nativity. The etymological meaning of *depraved* as crooked, distorted or perverse, suggests the sense of a wrong *direction* (always associated in Eliot's mind with the birth of Humanism); while its common usage links it with all the other images in the poem of debased or unnatural propagation. The Renaissance seemed a fresh flowering and illumination of human sense and spirit, bringing, as it were, the stars of the dogwood and the candles of the chestnut into the forests of the night. But it was 'flowering judas.' The new paganism betrayed the tiger, bringing not communion but division. The clear 'word' has lost all its resonance and is only a confusion of 'whispers.' In the place of a society nourished by the sacrament in which man could partake of the creative source of light and life (the Christ-mass), Gerontion sees four figures typical of his own deprivation of both spiritual and physical vitality. They are cosmopolitan, rootless and sapless creatures, cut off entirely from the lifeblood of a living tradition. To Mr. Silvero, Limoges enamels are simply objects of art; it is their surface texture only that interests him; his 'caressing hands' have nothing to

---

[1] *A Dialogue on Modern Poetry.* London. Oxford University Press, 1939.

do with a loving heart. Hakagawa's ritual among the Titians again ignores the tradition which has inspired the art. To Madame de Tornquist faith has degenerated to spiritualistic séances: Fraulein von Kulp has repudiated it, turning away from the door. This is probably to be too specific in interpretation, but more important is the emotional atmosphere suggested by the very precise gestures, which are all we are allowed to see of these people. They suggest restless loneliness, empty formality, dimness, evasion, doubt, uncertainty, frustration. They are summed up by the image of complete futility: 'Vacant shuttles/Weave the wind.'

Now the rhythm changes again. In opposition to 'the word within a word, unable to speak a word' is Gerontion's impassioned rhetoric of 'inquisition' on the subject of 'history.' It is strongly flavored by the use of language and the verse movement of the later Jacobean dramatists. But the parallel is not just stylistic. Style is the embodiment of a way of thinking and feeling, and with the manner, Eliot injects into the poem the quality of perception which linked him (or Gerontion) with the dramatists of the early seventeenth century. They too were alive in a period when the established beliefs in a religion of 'revelation' had been challenged by the autonomy of the individual intellect, resulting in a deep cleavage between the religious and the secular. They too felt a profound disgust at the society they pictured, living its 'depraved' life. They too in their poetry, married intellect and sense in a magnificent riot of creative zest, but it too was 'flowering judas' and brought no *human* fulfilment. Their tragedies also 'multiply variety in a wilderness of mirrors,' but end in much the same indiscriminate destruction as Eliot's poem.

But here, instead of the creation of the situation in dramatic flesh and blood figures working out their own destruction and that of their victims in terms of action, Eliot analyzes the interaction of elements in 'history' as a structure of symbols. 'History' is human experience lived without the framework of a Logos; lived by the 'knowledge' supplied by empirical science. It is man relying on his own desires and 'whispers,' believing that he can control his own fate; directed only by arbitrary expediency, inspired only by instinctive action and reaction in the world of temporal fate and change.

'After such knowledge what forgiveness?' *Forgiveness* must have an extended etymology here. What has man been given over to, or given up to, or resigned himself to, as the result of experience lived in these terms? The 'giving' and 'forgiving' are then played out in a series of images suggesting the 'depraved,' crooked ways of knowledge (cunning), the ways of self-deception and self-interest, their methods of propagation and what they propagate. Man craves knowledge (of himself, of truth), but history presents it 'when our attention is distracted,' when we are looking in a different direction, or are in a state of conflict, torn in opposing directions.

> And what she gives, gives with such supple confusions
> That the giving famishes the craving.

A wonderful creation in terms of sense of the intellectual struggle between faith and doubt. Then Gerontion seems to describe his own position towards religion's revelation. It becomes an experience at second hand:

> if still believed
> In memory only, reconsidered passion.

The alternative to that is the sentimental interpretation, which ignores hard realities 'till the refusal propagates a fear.' The earlier images of depraved and Judas propagation now shape and colour the ideas. Historical cause and effect are seen in terms of this 'spawning.' The statement is quite general, but in the actual historical context of the poem, linked with the opening paragraph, the 'unnatural vices' fathered by the heroisms of war become the financial operations of the 'owner' of the house, and the virtues 'forced upon us by our impudent crimes,' such things as submission and poverty or dependence—of no moral value if imposed by necessity. This is the 'forgiveness' resulting from the 'givings' of history: not a forgiveness based on love, but a world given over to conflict and confusion. 'These tears are shaken from the wrath-bearing tree': the fruit of the propagation is that of the Poison Tree of Blake's poem, watered with fears and tears, sunned with smiles and 'soft deceitful wiles,' and bearing only the death-dealing apple of destruction.

Into this vision of depraved human appetites and impotencies bursts the reminder that the tiger is eternally present. 'The tiger springs in the new year. Us he devours.' Christ as symbol of creative love, willing to share his body and blood with mankind and so making all men members one of another, is 'unable to speak a word.' But the logos remains as inexorable natural law, a 'fearful symmetry,' and the alternative to acceptance of it is destruction by it. Gerontion recognizes this, but he refuses to accept the direct, unequivocal truth of it. He shifts and palters as his 'dry brain' pursues its analysis of his own attitude in a kind of hopeless and half-hearted self-justification. He pleads that he is a passive victim: he is in the power of the 'owner'; the purpose of his 'show' is not to urge a return to old superstitions; it is a real effort to face the facts: 'I would meet you upon this honestly.' Speaking for, and of, the whole development of civilization since the Renaissance in terms of relationship to the central Christian symbol, he says:

> I that was near your heart was removed therefrom
> To lose beauty in terror, terror in inquisition.

The word *inquisition* implies the overtone of torture in his condition and it is set against the full meaning of *passion* in the Christian context. Intellectual scrutiny is compared with the 'beauty' of the concept which unites all men in their whole emotional being with 'the word' commemorated in the Crucifixion and the Communion. But faith cannot be commanded. Even the 'terror' of the sense of isolation is now lost. Again Gerontion excuses himself for his incapacity to experience passion:

> Why should I need to keep it
> Since what is kept must be adulterated?

The simplicity of the old faith must in any case be modified by new scientific investigation. But again in *adulterated* Eliot fuses the two ideas of the debasing and dishonouring as well as the diluting of the mythical vision by rational materialism.

In the next lines the abstract condition of 'inquisition' is again translated into active sensuous embodiment and movement. Gerontion is ironically aware that his analyses are profitless. They are 'chilled delirium.' There is no warmth and substance to them, and in the precise sense of delirium they are a wandering from the track. Compared with the spontaneous intuition of human communion and community, they are like a palate whipped up with pungent sauces beside natural appetite. Or they 'multiply variety in a wilderness of mirrors,' reflecting the bewildering disintegration and empty desolation of a vision cut off from any central source of light.

> What will the spider do,
> Suspend its operations, will the weevil
> Delay?

Will 'deliberations' stop 'conclusions'? Will the spider, spinning its money web, 'suspend its operations' in the financial markets? Will the inevitable cycle of moral cause and effect be halted, any more than the course of destructive nature?

The poem sweeps without pause to the answer in terms of visionary ruin. In contrast to the movement through cunning passages and contrived corridors and issues, to that of the thousand small deliberations and the refractions from a wilderness of mirrors, there are two clear, unequivocal images of cataclysmic violence. First the vision of the single blast in which the cosmopolitan, rootless society is

> Whirled
> Beyond the circuit of the shuddering Bear
> In fractured atoms.

Then the pathetic weakness of the innocent individual who will perish with the guilty, appears as the single gull, helplessly buffeting the wind and finally hurled by it downwards to the desolation of 'white feathers in the snow, the Gulf claims.' The Trades turn into the devouring tempest, and the Gulf claims the old man himself. The 'show' ends; Gerontion proposes no *action* which can prevent the inexorable end. He reveals his 'thoughts' to his fellow 'tenants' and leaves his warning with them. The final images of drought and sterility lead directly to the atmosphere of *The Waste Land*.

CHAPTER V

❖❖❖

The Waste Land

> We work in the dark—we do what we can—we give
> what we have. Our doubt is our passion and our passion
> is our task. The rest is the madness of art.
>
> HENRY JAMES. *The Middle Years*

I DISLIKE the word "generation." When I wrote a poem
called *The Waste Land* some of the more approving critics
said that I had expressed "the disillusionment of a generation," which is nonsense. I may have expressed for them their
own illusion of being disillusioned, but that did not form part
of my intention.' [1]

Eliot's irritation at such criticism is natural. The poem, like
Sweeney among the Nightingales or *Gerontion,* is visionary and
timeless, and the 'figure in the carpet' which is woven through
it has been woven through centuries of general and personal
experience in a changeless pattern. The very number of cultures
and languages and of associations with the experiences of
other poets which are absorbed into the structure is enough to
suggest its universality. Nor is 'disillusionment' a possible word
to apply to Eliot, since it implies some 'illusion' held before, of
which there is never any trace in his poetry. Perhaps, however,
there was some excuse for the early readers of the poem. It
is of the essence of Eliot's method that the experiences created
and enacted in his poems are both timeless and timely, but the
most obvious element in the early poems is the immediate sense
of the ugliness, the emptiness and the aimlessness of the contemporary world. In *The Waste Land,* the means by which

[1] *Thoughts after Lambeth.* Selected Essays.

this is seen as one element only in a larger composition, cannot be clarified without the study of external sources; and the subtle shift in psychological attitude which characterizes the poem, is also obscured by the extreme complexity of his method.

Eliot referred his readers to his external sources in his notes at the end of the poem.

> Not only the title, but the plan and a good deal of the incidental symbolism of the poem were suggested by Miss Jessie L. Weston's book on the Grail legend: *From Ritual to Romance*. Indeed, so deeply am I indebted, Miss Weston's book will elucidate the difficulties of the poem much better than my notes can do; and I recommend it . . . to any who think such elucidation of the poem worth the trouble. To another work of anthropology I am indebted in general, one which has influenced our generation profoundly; I mean *The Golden Bough;* I have used especially the two volumes *Adonis, Attis, Osiris*. Anyone who is acquainted with these works will immediately recognize in the poem certain references to vegetation ceremonies.

It may be argued that it is asking a good deal of the readers of poetry that they should study several books on anthropology before being equipped to read a poem fully, just as it may be argued that it requires a good deal of any reader to attempt to follow out other sources of Eliot's imaginative processes. The only answer to this is that there is no compulsion on anyone to read either poetry or anthropology, unless they feel 'elucidation of the poem worth the trouble.' But it is true that the effort at elucidation has of necessity been slow. The range of reference is so wide, and to most readers so unfamiliar, and it is so deeply integrated into a complex psychological situation. The parallel between past and present never really comes to the surface—which is as it should be—for the poem would lose in intensity if its course were simplified. But it is true that to the majority of readers, before that intensity can be fully appreciated as an experience of poetry, the intellectual background has to be absorbed and the logical links explained. There are readers who think rational elucidation detracts from the poetic experience and is unnecessary. I. A. Richards called *The Waste Land* 'a music of ideas' and said that 'the ideas, like the musician's phrases, are arranged not that they may tell us something, but that their effects in us may combine into a coherent whole of feeling and attitude.' Structurally, in its use of themes, the poem is allied to music, but 'a music of ideas' implies an analogy which is not very satisfactory, for the simple reason that ideas, expressed verbally, are not musical phrases. Their combinations are not those of sound only but of sense. Unless they did 'tell us something' they could not combine into 'a coherent whole of feeling and attitude.' Moreover, it is a justifiable ambition to want to know what the poet is feeling about and what he is holding an attitude towards. Indeed until we know these things we can hardly judge whether the poem coheres.

A reading of *From Ritual to Romance* and *The Golden Bough* certainly gives us many clues as to 'the continuous parallel between contemporaneity and antiquity' which Eliot is manipulating.[2] Miss Weston's book deals with the origins of the Grail legend, and its puzzling and apparently irreconcilable elements of paganism and Christianity. The legend appears in various confusing forms in medieval literature, but it always concerns a land which has been blighted by a curse so that it is arid and waterless, producing neither animal nor vegetable increase. Its plight is linked with that of its ruler, the Fisher King, who, as a result of illness or of a wound, has become sexually impotent. The curse is removed when a Knight ap-

[2] The first critic to work this out in detail was Cleanth Brooks in *Modern Poetry and the Tradition*.

pears who must ask the question as to the meaning of the Grail and the Lance—said in Christian terms to be the lance which pierced Christ's side at the Crucifixion, and the cup from which he and the disciples drank at the Last Supper. In some versions the mere asking of the question cures the King and saves the land. In others the knight must go through various ordeals, culminating in that of the Chapel or Cemetery Perilous. Miss Weston, using her own researches and those of other scholars, finds the legends to be Christianized versions of beliefs which go back to immemorial antiquity. She traces their origins to a common source in the vegetation rituals and fertility rites of primitive cultures, and the 'mystery' religions of the ancient world, from which early Christianity absorbed so much of its own ritual and symbolism.

The Sumerian-Babylonian god Tammuz, the Phoenician-Greek Adonis, the Phrygian Attis and the Egyptian Osiris were all expressions of the primitive imagination which conceived of the cycle of the seasons as the life of a god who controlled the energies of nature, and who nevertheless had to submit to the power of death. But the death was not permanent, it was followed by a resurrection. The worship of the god was accompanied by ritual observances and alternate ceremonies of mourning and rejoicing. And since water was the basic necessity to these agricultural communities, the resurrection of the god coincided with the coming of the spring rains, the central symbol of the fertilizing process. But these early vegetation myths developed later into the 'mystery religions,' which linked the ideas of death and resurrection in the natural world with that of a parallel process in the world of the spirit. Membership in the religious body was prefaced by initiation rites, which were analogous to those practiced by primitive peoples at the age of puberty. Malinowski states that all such ceremonies have broadly the same characteristics and functions. The youth passes through a series of ordeals, which are usually associated with the idea of death and rebirth, which is sometimes enacted in a mimetic performance. Besides the ordeals, however, and in reality more important, is the instruction in the sacred myths and traditions and the unveiling of the tribal mysteries which relate the individual to higher and unseen powers and personalities. In this way the rites symbolize not only a biological and social coming of age, but also a spiritual metamorphosis.

In the mystery cults of the ancient world, just as in the fertility rituals, water played a very important part in the initiation ceremonies. They included some form of immersion or baptism. But they went beyond any mere external ceremony. Miss Weston thinks the candidates enacted some symbolic rite of death and resurrection, involving stern tests of physical and mental endurance, which, if successful, led the initiate to a sense of union with the life-principle itself. Certainly the various trials in these rites were very severe, sometimes costing the reason of those who took part in them.

Miss Weston traces the origin of the Grail legend to the early Christian sect of the Gnostics, later proclaimed heretical by the Early Church. The central tenet of the Gnostics was that the Christ was the consummation of the inner spiritual meaning of all the earlier 'mysteries,' the symbol of the mediator between man and the supreme source of spiritual life, through whose worship knowledge of and union with that life could be attained. The Gnostics, she thinks, as they travelled into Western Europe, transposed the older symbols into their Christian forms, making the Lance and the Grail part of the Christian story, instead of having their old fertility significance as the male and female sex symbols. They likewise transposed the initiation ceremonies into the ordeals of the knights who set out to achieve the cure of the King and salvation for the land through self-purification.

It is these elements from the past, although the references to them in the poem are so oblique and so interwoven with symbolism from other sources, which provide Eliot with the plan, with 'a way of controlling and ordering and giving shape and significance to the immense panorama of fertility and anarchy which is contemporary history.' And it is evident from the nature of the material to which his mind responded at this time, that it was deeply involved in a new direction. His inspiration is a book about the immemorial antiquity of the search for union with the source of inner vitality. The legend hovering behind it is that of the need to question what the source of this vitality is, the need to set out on a quest for its recovery, and to undertake the necessary disciplines involved in that quest. Other 'ghosts' haunting the poem are Shakespeare's *The Tempest,* with its central metaphor of being 'sea-swallowed,' and regenerated from that experience; Dante's *Purgatorio;* Buddha and St. Augustine as preachers of asceticism, and a legend from an Upanishad giving moral instruction.

All this is very different from the atmosphere of *Gerontion.* There the whole vision is that of death-in-life and of the physical annihilation which will conclude it. The life-giving 'sign' remains 'the word within a word unable to speak a word.' In *The Waste Land,* too, one of the elements is the blindness and numbness of the external contemporary consciousness; its sterility, impotence, emptiness and aridity; its general loss of any vital relationship with the language of symbols, and in general with the human heritage of tradition. Everything which once spoke to man of the deepest realities and mysteries of his being, has become rationalized and vulgarized and sterilized of its inner content into a mere shell of inorganic materialism. But to the 'I' of the poem the ancient 'word' is no longer completely dumb and dark. He no longer says 'I have lost my passion.' He is agonizingly aware, in the imprisonment of his personal waste land, that the possibilities of rebirth cannot be dismissed as an historical anachronism; that the truth of the experience is eternally present and that the living of it plunges the whole man into a process of disintegration and conflict.

It is this aspect of the poem which can be related to Jung's 'archetype of transformation,' for he describes the opening of that drama in the life of any human being in terms which at once remind any reader of Eliot of the emotional situation created in *Gerontion* and *The Waste Land,* and the central dream-images are the same as those used by Eliot. As I emphasized before there is no need to accept Jung's theory of a collective unconscious to account for this. Eliot knew the sources of all his symbols and used them with all the conscious manipulation of the artist. His mind had already absorbed the whole literary and cultural tradition of Europe, as well as a great deal of Asiatic religion and philosophy. The point of comparison is simply *what* of all this 'comes together' in the poem, and the fact that at this period Eliot's mind responds to and relives certain symbols of imaginative experience recurrent in the whole human story.

Jung describes the process of 'transformation' as occurring to those who have reached a dead end in the field of conscious adaptation to external experience without however achieving any sense of fulfilment. There are therefore stores of unconscious psychic energy unutilized, while in the field of *consciousness* its creative function is exhausted. The result is the multitude of Mr. Silveros and Madame de Tornquists, in a condition of futile nervous disturbance. But there are also the Gerontions who are in the torture of 'inquisition;' who see their situation with merciless clarity but can find no way out of the cunning passages and contrived corridors. They are completely aware of their 'dryness,' their loss of communion with any life-giving source, but the situation cannot be altered in the terms in which they see it without a radical change in *themselves.* The 'I would meet you upon this honestly' attitude results only in the establishment of irreconcilable opposites, 'beauty' and 'inquisition,' which cannot be brought together.

Here, says Jung, 'we find ourselves outside the domain covered by the views of Freud and Adler, for we are no longer concerned with the question of how to deal with the obstacles that hinder a man in the practical expansion of his personal and social relationships. Instead we are confronted with the task of finding a meaning which will make possible the very continuance of life, in so far as it is to be more than mere resignation and mournful introspection.'[3] Jung's theory is that then the unused psychic potentialities in the unconscious 'activate a more or less primitive analogy of the conscious situation in the unconscious, together with an earlier mode of adaptation.'[4] This is thrown into consciousness in the form of the primordial images. But the dream symbols, though they contain the possibilities of a new adaptation and point to the presence of the forces which can help to bring it about, are always ambiguous and ambivalent. Their irruption into consciousness, though it brings the seed of new growth, means a disruption of the existing conscious pattern, and therefore on one side a disintegration and death. There is a longing for renewal of life and growth but at the same time a longing to escape it; mingled desire and fear, hope and despair. 'The collapse of the conscious attitude at first feels like the end of the world'; indeed images itself as such: 'quite at the beginning sometimes stands the cosmic catastrophe'—the Gulf 'claims' everything.

The dominating image always appears as that of water, having the ambiguity of all the primordial images in that it symbolizes means and ends of both life and death, and both as inseparable parts of one process. In this context, as the first phase of 'transformation,' it symbolizes to Jung the unconscious itself, the depths of himself through which a man must descend before rising again; or the depths in which he fishes for the answers to his riddles. But it is the symbol too of 'the

[3] *Two Essays on Analytical Psychology*, p. 76.
[4] *Psychological Types*, p. 231.

way of initiation,' of the possible transformation. 'Manifestly, primitive initiations are transformation mysteries of the greatest psychic significance.' [5] In particular he sees the original concept symbolized into the ritual of baptism as one of the great milestones in the history of man. It meant that his development had risen to the level of the idea that the 'natural man' *could* be transcended; that there was another dimension of being into which he could be born. Jung sees all primitive initiations as the original objectifications of this psychic process of metamorphosis, felt afresh by every individual who *lives* the experience behind the symbols, and given new forms by the creative artist in the terms of his own personal vision.

In his memorial lecture on Yeats, Eliot says that the great poet is the man who 'out of intense and personal experience is able to express a general truth: retaining all the particularity of his experience to make it a general symbol.' This is what *The Waste Land* does. The presence of sterile *de*generation and the necessity of *re*generation and change is the general truth behind it and its central theme. But there is nothing clear-cut and simple about this experience in the life of the individual. Spring does not follow winter in an orderly rhythmical sequence in the psychic world. To be 'born again of water and the spirit' is as momentous and crucial an experience as the psychologists now tell us human birth is to the infant; with the difference that to the adult is added all its conscious problems in the worlds of moral choice and action, and all its desperate conflicts between belief and doubt. Moreover, the experience is additionally complex and difficult in the midst of a society in which all the traditions of Western civilization in which it has been symbolized have become 'undecipherable.' *The Waste Land* is the translation of all this into the language of poetry; a dramatization of the struggles of the poet in this

[5] *Two Essays on Analytical Psychology*, p. 256.

situation, created through the use of symbolic transformations. The background of anthropology and the evocation of the past through the allusions to its literature give us the clues, but it is their rhythmic inter-relationships with Eliot's own use of language which give us the poetry.

The notes give valuable help with the references, but not much else. Eliot does however tell us that the figure of Tiresias 'although a mere spectator and not indeed a "character," is yet the most important personage in the poem, uniting all the rest. Just as the one-eyed merchant, seller of currants, melts into the Phoenician Sailor, and the latter is not wholly distinct from Ferdinand Prince of Naples, so all the women are one woman, and the two sexes meet in Tiresias. What Tiresias *sees* in fact is the substance of the poem.' But Tiresias is blind, so the ancient seer seems therefore to represent the eye of the mind, a universal contemplative consciousness, almost 'the historical sense' itself. As such, it is the inner reality which subsists through all experience that he *sees,* which unites past and present, men and women, the 'characters' in the poem and the 'I' who is its mouthpiece.

The structure of the poem is built up of contrasts, of which the most obvious and ironically dramatic are the series of 'scenes' from modern life, set against the memories of the myths related in *From Ritual to Romance* and *The Golden Bough,* and supported by the suggestions evoked by Eliot's vast store of literary reminiscence. But interwoven with these, so that the two constantly 'melt into' one another, are the passages of drama on the psychological level, the conflicts and contrasts of mood, which again in their turn interpenetrate and interfuse. The whole experience is prefaced by an epigraph from the *Satyricon* of Petronius where a drunken scoffer is deriding the heroic past. He speaks of the Cumaean Sibyl, most famous of prophetesses, to whom Apollo granted a life of as many years as she had grains of dust in her hand. But she forgot to ask for eternal youth, and so shrivelled to

nothing. Here the speaker claims he has seen her, hanging in a
jar, and that when her acolytes asked: 'What do you want?'
she replied: 'I want to die.' The quotation reflects both the
scornful attitude of the contemporary world towards 'tradition,'
and the despairing personal death-wish which is one aspect of
the poem's emotional pattern. Its opposite is the conclusion, the
answer to a different questioning about life, the recognition
of the peace which may be the result of the willing acceptance of a symbolic death and a discipline of directed
action. This peace is not achieved in the poem, but its appearance as a possibility is its most important psychological content.
The psychic drama of the whole is enclosed within these two
conflicting visions.

The conflict is present in the opening lines, where in image,
rhythm and association the themes are given their first statement. Nature awakens to new life and fertility in its eternal
cycle; the 'shoures swete' hailed by Chaucer have come. But
this is no glad welcome to the spring. The poet's feeling
towards both winter and April, towards the suspension of life
in which he is living, and towards a rebirth, is ambivalent,
'mixing memory and desire.' One impulse of both memory and
desire is towards the apathy and oblivion of winter. The possibility of renewal, the thought of being stirred into potency
and growth, the compulsion towards it felt in the rhythm of
the first four lines, are mated and mingled with a fear and
reluctance which drive him back to safe forgetfulness. Then,
without transition, there is a sudden change to a rhythm of
release and lightness. It is an escape, but into what? Into a
world where seasons are only a matter of scenery and sports
and travel, of rain and sunlight on mountain or valley, of
the light superficial chatter of rootless, cosmopolitan tourists,
rolling stones who are no part of the rhythm of the life-cycle.
These are some of the inhabitants of the Waste Land. There is

no release among them, and in the sonorous rhythm of biblical echoes, the poet asks his first question and is answered cryptically in terms of doom. The myths of the ancient world are 'a heap of broken images'; the desert is waterless. The passage in *Ecclesiastes* to which Eliot refers us, tells of the coming of death 'when fears shall be in the way . . . and desire shall fail: because man goeth to his long home . . . Then shall the dust return to earth as it was.' The next lines are very elusive. In contrast to the 'stony rubbish,' the prophet says:

> Only
> There is shadow under this red rock,
> (Come in under the shadow of this red rock),
> And I will show you something different from either
> Your shadow at morning striding behind you
> Or your shadow at evening rising to meet you;
> I will show you fear in a handful of dust.

There seems to be an ironic echo of Isaiah: 'And a man shall be as the shadow of a great rock in a weary land, as rivers of water in a dry place.' But the redness of the rock remains rather baffling. May it be a reference to the Mount of Purgatory reddened by the setting sun in Canto III of the *Purgatorio?* Dante notices that his figure casts a shadow on the rock while that of Virgil does not. Virgil tells him that he casts no shadow because he no longer has a body. If we wrest a gloss from this it would be that to accept purgatory while still in the body, to 'come in under the shadow of this red rock' would in one way be to become 'fear in a handful of dust.' But it would be different from the living death of the monotonous empty round of

> Your shadow at morning striding behind you
> Or your shadow at evening rising to meet you.

A handful of dust moreover, though it may be a synonym for death can become fruitful soil with the help of 'spring rain.'

But there may be no literary reference at all. We may read it purely in terms of emotion and sensation. First the desert scene in all its parching heat and drought; then the hope and longing for relief and shade; the mocking invitation to come and find something different from the loneliness and emptiness; and finally the sardonic revelation of human reality without the shadow giving it the shape of a man: 'fear in a handful of dust.'

There is the same collapse into the deadening sense of paralyzed hope in the next sequence. As the water image breaks in, the rhythm breaks into buoyancy with the fragment of the sailor's song in the first act of *Tristan and Isolde,* 'the wind blows fresh from the homeland, where are you lingering?' But the passage ends with a line from the third act, 'empty and blank the sea,' sung as Tristan lies dying and there is no sign of Isolde's ship. The sea proves traitor; it is the *arrest* of consummation, its collapse into the waste of waters, which remains. And between the two quotations is the suggestion of another frustrated love, an arrested spring, a thwarted fulfil-ment. The Hyacinth garden brings the reminder of a fertility festival; the picture of the girl that of spring and abundance and an exquisite promise. But the conclusion is the torture of a vision seen and felt, with the power of creative response, of speech, movement, interpretation, withheld. From a refer-ence in the notes to the next section, which connects this pas-sage also with *The Tempest,* I think we are meant to have a memory of Ferdinand and Miranda; of Prospero striking Ferdinand into immobility by a spell, and his remark 'My spirits, as in a dream, are all bound up.'

The thrusting forward of the life-cycle in the opening lines of the poem has had no parallel in the life of the spirit. There we have seen only the trivial tourists, the successive symbols of drought and death and the frustration of any consummation. With the entrance of Madame Sosostris and her 'wicked pack of cards' we move to another variation of the life-death theme, coloured by mingling tones of satiric 'levity' and serious signifi-cance. We move too into an area of the poem where the con-temporary scene must be juxtaposed to its parallel in the past. For Madame Sosostris, with her name suggesting a Greek-Egyptian origin, is a modern, vulgarized version of the Egyp-tian diviners and practicers of magic, who professed to control fertility, and to forecast the rising and falling of the waters of the Nile through the Tarot cards. But she is no longer con-cerned with the ancient magic which sought to control the sources of life. What originated in a technique of mastery has become a masquerade. Her reality is dead and she prac-tices her shady fortune-telling in an atmosphere of fear of the police: 'One must be so careful these days.' She has a bad cold—her voice is muffled and unclear. Her message too is equally so! But she introduces us to characters and themes which are developed later, and comments on them with the patter of her trade, while their true significance is unknown to her. The protagonist's card is the drowned Phoenician sailor, and hence she tells him to 'fear death by water.' But the sailor is later a symbol of the effigy of Adonis put into the sea at Alexandria and carried by the current to Byblos and there welcomed with rejoicing as the promise of the rebirth of spring. His 'drowning' is also a symbol of baptism, so Madame Sosostris' warning is solely on the level of the destructive pos-sibilities hidden in the water symbol. One of those is the drowning in the shallow waters of the suffocating contemporary atmosphere, the 'human voices wake us and we drown,' of Mr. Prufrock. Another is the psychological death-wish. Yet another, I think, is the temptation to drown out the moral and spiritual problems of the personal life by the creative activity of art alone. This is borne out by the quotation from *The Tempest* which follows the introduction of the sailor symbol '(Those are pearls that were his eyes).' We know that that quotation and the lines that follow it in Ariel's song, are associated in Eliot's mind with the transmuting of life into art.[6] But the quotation stands for much more than that. It is the central symbol in the poem for the whole process of metamorphosis in both its destructive and creative aspects. In the first, it points to the change of the living symbols of the past into inanimate, inorganic, matter; the vision commemorated in the whole Western tradition has become opaque and lifeless as the pearl—which again is a disease in the life of the oyster. But in its creative aspect, Ariel's song reminds us of a supposed death by drowning which in reality led to a regeneration through 'sea change,' and a metamorphosis from blindness to new vision.

Belladonna, the Lady of the Rocks, presumably symbolizes the quality of all the women in the poem. Like the woman in *Gerontion*, they are all the antithesis of the idea of fertility. Her name suggests poison and the numbing of sensitivity, coupled with the aridity of rocks and a preference for 'situations' instead of fruitful union. Eliot tells us that the man with three staves stands for the Fisher King himself, and the Wheel is the common symbol of cyclic pattern, which also appears again in the 'Death by Water' section. Cleanth Brooks suggests that the merchant is one-eyed because he is in profile on the card, though later, as we shall see, that too has a further significance. What he carries on his back is the secret of the mystery cults, which were spread all over the ancient world by the Syrian traders. Eliot tells us that the Hanged Man is associated in his mind with the Hanged God of Frazer, a myth of sacrificial death, and with the hooded figure in the passage of the disciples to Emmaus in Part V. He is not found in the world of Madame Sosostris.

The 'crowds of people, walking round in a ring' form the transition to the final death theme of Part I, the horror of

---

[6] See the reference to Coleridge's *Kubla Khan* on p. 21, and to the struggles of the poet on p. 31.

life in the modern city. The city was a maternal symbol to the ancients, but it is now utterly barren. It is 'unreal' because it is cut off from both natural and spiritual sources of life, and because it no longer has anything of its old sense of 'community.' Each individual exists in drab loneliness, and the mass, 'flowing' over the bridge has no more human identity than the river flowing under it. It is 'unreal' too because it is indeterminate in its mantle of brown fog, and finally, because, like Baudelaire's Paris, it has taken on the character of a scene in a nightmare, 'where the spectre in broad daylight stops the passer by.' The figures are like those in Dante's Limbo, who were never baptized, or those in the anteroom to Hell, 'those wretches who never were alive; who lived without praise or blame'; the neutrals, the Mrs. Equitones. Their plight, in Dante, is that as they denied life, so 'they have no hope of death.' The church clock 'with a dead sound on the final stroke of nine,' the ninth hour of the Crucifixion, brings no such memories to the inhabitants of the Unreal City. It is almost impossible not to let the associations spread further here. The reference which Eliot gives us to Book III of the *Inferno* for the line 'I had not thought death had undone so many,' is followed immediately by the description of one 'who made, through cowardice, the great refusal.' During the next passage this figure seems to merge with Baudelaire's spectre and the passer by, with Stetson and the protagonist, and by extension through the mention of Mylae, to all those who are called upon at all times and in all places to fight all kinds of battles. In the last line it includes also the 'hypocrite reader' and the poet himself. All these are tempted to 'the great refusal,' and torn between the living death of the Waste Land and that surrender to the symbolic death which may bring rebirth.

The agonized address to Stetson takes us back to the winter-spring statement of the theme in the opening lines. 'That corpse you planted last year in your garden' is a reference to the myth of Osiris as the corn god. Frazer tells us that at the yearly festival of the sowing of the grain, the priests used to bury effigies of the god made of earth and corn. 'When these effigies were taken up again . . . the corn would be found to have sprouted from the body and this would be hailed as the cause of the growth of the crops. The corn god produced the corn from himself: He gave his own body to feed the people: he died that they might live.'[7] But the tortured questioning of the protagonist has again the inextricably intertwined attraction and repulsion of the opening lines. His imagination is filled with a medley of fleeting associations, catching up images already used, adding new ones, concentrating suggestions, and bursting into an intense semi-hysterical horror and confusion of response, as he is forced to face 'the cruellest month' and its implications. Will the metamorphosis from death to life take place or has the chill of cowardice blighted its growth? The next couplet

> Oh keep the Dog far hence, that's friend to men,
> Or with his nails he'll dig it up again!

takes us to a dirge sung over a corpse in Webster's *White Devil*. There, the poet calls to

> The ant, the field mouse and the mole
> To rear him hillocks that shall keep him warm,

and we already know that 'winter kept us warm' and that winter symbolizes the living death of the Waste Land itself. The song continues: 'But keep the wolf far thence, that's foe to men'—Eliot's changes in the text carry on the anguished ambivalence of attitudes. The dog was a common symbol of aid to rebirth. Isis collected the pieces of the dismembered

---

[7] *The Golden Bough,* abridged edition, p. 376.

corpse of Osiris with the aid of dogs.[8] Or again, if the capitalization means the Dog star, Sirius, who was herald of the rising of the Nile waters, he would be 'friend to man' in the truest sense, 'stirring dull roots with spring rain,' and when the corpse was dug up it would have sprouted. Maybe there's a hint of the Hound of Heaven, and that the 'nails' associate the Osiris myth with the Crucifixion. In any case the total emotional effect is that of an equal horror towards the living death of the crowd flowing over the bridge and the alternative of facing the cruel 'breeding' that could bring fresh life.

The second part, 'A Game of Chess,' deals directly with the artificiality and lack of human or mythical meaning in the central 'fertility' situation, the marriage relation of men and women. It opens with a reminiscence of Cleopatra, but the vitality of the contemporary women in the dramatic glimpses that follow is as that of queens on a chessboard compared with that on the 'burnished throne' of Egypt, and their 'games' with men are nothing but an empty pastime or an open hostility ending in a stalemate. This is underlined by Eliot's note referring us to Middleton's play *Women beware Women* with its chessplaying scene. There the game is used to distract the attention of a simple woman while the Duke seduces her daughter-in-law, and the seduction is described ironically in terms of the moves of the pieces on the board. (The whole play, indeed, is nothing but a battle of sexual intrigue, where piece after piece falls to the manoeuvres of the opponents until finally death checkmates all.) The oppositions in the poem are superficially those of a woman's room, (created in the most lavish and luxuriant profusion of sense impressions, and preparing the reader instinctively to hear of a passion which

[8] See also Petronius' *Satyricon*, c. 71, 'I beseech you to fasten beside the feet of my statue a dog, so that because of your beneficence I may attain to life after death.'

matches the richness of its setting), with two dramatic dialogues illustrating two aspects of the terrible emotional barrenness of the modern world. In each the woman could well be described as 'the Lady of the Rocks, the Lady of Situations,' for both give a picture where any fruitful relationship is absent. Within the large contrasting oppositions the psychological themes of the first part appear too.

There is no need to analyze the brilliance of the descriptive passage, with its loaded intensification of sensuous opulence and prodigality, its sensual imagery, and its echoes from Shakespeare and Virgil to create the memory of Cleopatra and Dido, two queens who chose death rather than life without love. It is the startling intrusion of the word *synthetic,* in the description of the perfumes which

> troubled, confused
> And drowned the sense in odours

that prepares us for the atmosphere of the artificial and unnatural which is to colour the following scene. In the man and woman playing their tragedy of negative frustration in this voluptuous setting we are once more to be in the living death of the Waste Land. But before we pass to that, we have a glimpse, through a picture on the wall, of the central theme of metamorphosis. 'As though a window gave upon the sylvan scene,' the poet evokes

> The change of Philomel, by the barbarous king
> So rudely forced; yet there the nightingale
> Filled all the desert with inviolable voice

There, in that world where the physical and temporal is transcended by the spiritual and eternal, her song gave meaning to her mortal pain. But she does not sing in the desert places of the present. *Here* lust still triumphs, her voice is vulgarized, and the sustained sweetness of the last line quoted above collapses into the tired disgust of ' "Jug Jug" to dirty ears.' The picture is now meaningless, the fresh sylvan scene turns to 'withered stumps of time.' The vision of an opening window, and of the 'stony rubbish' of the Waste Land being filled with eternal song, is darkened and silenced.

> staring forms
> Leaned out, leaning, hushing the room enclosed.

The inescapable nightmare of the present overshadows and imprisons all. The rich associations of light, colour, movement and perfume which the fertile verbal magic and fluid rhythms of the opening passage have aroused, fade out into elliptical, uneven lines, where the woman's hair, her mood as she brushes it, and her voice, all share the syntax to create the atmosphere of compressed nervous tension. This mounts through the abrupt realistic dialogue that follows, and the atmosphere of dead negation invades and envelopes the room. Again there is questioning; staccato, insistent, nagging, and the answers bring images of death, nothingness, the horror of annihilation, the sound of the empty wind under the door. Through this the melody of the song of 'sea-change' breaks, 'Those are pearls that were his eyes,' but only as a mockery in a meaningless ragtime. Now it is only a shred of memory of the life-giving symbol, which is powerless to assert itself in the world where water means only

> The hot water at ten
> And if it rains, a closed car at four.

A world 'enclosed' like that of the chessboard; a world where the 'staring forms' cannot be shut out, and where the 'shuffling footsteps on the stair' will end only by death's knock on the door.

The knocking on the door is the bridge to the next scene with the beat of its ominous refrain 'HURRY UP PLEASE

IT's TIME'—the pub-keeper announcing the closing hour. If any choice is to be made, it must be before the final goodnight makes it too late. But the women in the pub are also in a 'room enclosed.' Their Cockney voices are the only melody within the refrain; vulgar, insensitive voices which speak of marriage, unfaithfulness, fertility and abortion at exactly the same level and in exactly the same tone as of a set of new teeth or a Sunday dinner. Abortion, the deliberate destruction of life, has meaning only in terms of spoiling a woman's looks. The word *antique,* echoed from the 'antique mantel' above which 'the change of Philomel' was displayed, brings here no memory of antiquity and its glories. They are as faded as the woman's face. The goodnights of the group modulate into the voice of the mad Ophelia, the preface to another death by drowning, but a death which is self-destruction, the end of frustrated love, not a baptism and regeneration into a new birth.

In the Fire Sermon, the Buddha tells the assembled priests that all things are on fire, all things received as impressions through the senses or through the mind. 'And with what are they on fire?' ask the priests. The Blessed One replies: 'With the fire of passion, with the fire of hatred, with the fire of infatuation; with birth, old age, death, sorrow, lamentation, misery, grief and despair are they on fire.' The way of the disciple is to turn from the world, to become 'free from attachment.' The 'fire' described in this, with the quotation from St. Augustine, 'To Carthage then I came, where a cauldron of unholy loves sang all about mine ears,' are the background of this part of the poem.

At the opening, the memory of Spenser's marriage song and its scenes of nymphs and lovers preparing gaily for a wedding on the riverbank, haunt the picture of autumn desolation; but the scene is no *more* desolate than that of the pollution of the stream by the modern promiscuous lovers of the summer nights. Then the theme of exile, of waters that can do nothing to slake the longing for release, sounds in the line, 'By the waters of Leman I sat down and wept . . .,' where the Babylonian captivity is interwoven with that of the Prisoner of Chillon. The wind 'unheard' before, turns to a cold blast bringing first the contrapuntal melody of Marvell. But the sound of 'Time's winged chariot' and the vision of 'deserts of vast eternity,' are contracted to the rattle of the bones and of the grinning death's head, 'the chuckle spread from ear to ear.' Spenser's river and the sea in *The Tempest* shrink to 'the dull canal,' the Grail Castle to the gashouse. The protagonist, the Fisher King and Ferdinand melt into a single figure. But no magic creeps by upon the waters, telling of a sea change. Only the slimy rat 'crept softly through the vegetation'; the bodies seen do not lie 'full fathom five,' but 'naked on the low damp ground'; the bones are not turned to living coral. Nor are they those of the men who were 'sea-swallowed, though some cast again' into a new life: they are

> Cast into a little low dry garret
> Rattled by the rat's foot only, year to year.

Instead of the song luring Ferdinand towards Miranda, or the hunting horns bringing Actaeon to Diana, it is the horns of the motors which herald the loves of Sweeney and Mrs. Porter, and the fragment of a vulgar ballad. Into this breaks momentarily another music, that described by Verlaine, in his sonnet on Parsifal, the purity of children's voices singing of the Grail ritual. But that music cannot be sustained any more than that of Philomel's 'inviolable voice.' To 'dirty ears' it too is vulgarized. The brown fog of the city again darkens and distorts reality, and in it the protagonist meets Mr. Eugenides, the Smyrna merchant.

Of his counterpart in the ancient world, Miss Weston says:

'As ardently religious as practically business-like, the Syrians introduced their native deities wherever they penetrated, founding their chapels at the same time as their counting-houses.' But Mr. Eugenides now brings nothing but his merchandise; he is "one-eyed" because he has an eye to business only; his language is the ritual of commercial transactions. His invitation is to share promiscuous pleasures. His 'cult' may be (as Cleanth Brooks suggests) that of sexual perversion.

The next passage, the scene of the typist and 'the young man carbuncular,' may have behind it a similar implied parallel between past and present. On the superficial level it is one more example of the debased attitude towards sexual relations between men and women. It is part of the irony of the whole section that it is not the *fire* of lust at all which is illustrated, but merely the complete *indifference* towards chastity. But it may be that Eliot is also recalling what Frazer describes as the 'sanctified harlotry' of ancient rituals, by which, in order to promote fertility, a girl consorted with a stranger before marriage, the act being accompanied by a ritual feast and music. The introduction of Tiresias at this point, weaving his consciousness of the past through it all, points to two levels of meaning, and the flavour of debased ritual is caught and emphasized by the entrance of the formality of rhyme to describe its cheap tawdriness. It is a sort of ghastly parody of the fertility ritual, just as the evening home-coming of the city worker is a ghastly parody of Sappho's lines to the evening star, and Stevenson's *Requiem,* and her drying combinations 'out of the window perilously spread,' a mockery of the

> Magic casements, opening on the foam
> Of perilous seas. . . .

The line from Goldsmith again points the meaninglessness of the loss of chastity today, and the record on the gramophone— like the linking of the human heart with the throbbing of the taxi—emphasizes the automatic, mechanical nature of the sexual performance. The music and rhythm of love is degraded to this, and it is this music which accompanies the poet in the Unreal City.

But then there is a swift transition. The line from *The Tempest* takes on its true context, and we can imagine 'This music crept by me upon the waters' to be followed by

> Allaying both their fury and my passion
> With its sweet air.

'O City City' the poet cries, in distinction to the Unreal City. The city becomes for a moment the unit of public communal life, the Greek city, coloured by 'Ionian white and gold.' Its people are no longer a collection of neutral nonentities, the crowds 'walking round in a ring.' The public bar is no longer a 'room enclosed.' The rattle of the bones, the chuckle of the death's head, the sound of horns and motors and the mechanical gramaphone fade into

> The pleasant whining of a mandoline
> And a clatter and a chatter from within
> Where fishmen lounge at noon:

The fishmen have a *corporate* life, joined in a community and a harmony of work and relaxation, under the shadow of the church's beauty and splendour.

The river nymphs of the opening now change to the three Thames-daughters, whom Eliot associates with the Rhine-daughters of the *Götterdämmerung*. In Wagner's opera, the nymphs lament the change in the beauty of the Rhine since they have been robbed of the gold they guarded. Here the Thames-daughters compare the pollution of the river in the present day, and its sluggish movement and cluttered surface, with the colour and liveliness and music and brightness of the Elizabethan scene. The three violated Thames-daughters then sing separately, each telling her pitiful story. The first, echoing Dante's 'La Pia,' sets the scene in the Waste Land as a purgatory on earth—but a purgatory of no value since its suffering is not voluntary and purposive. Each singer treats her loss of chastity as inevitable and as bound up with the very soil of the Waste Land. The river or the sea at the scene of violation have no cleansing power. It is all meaningless; it is of no consequence; it has no *relation* to anything; it is part of the nothingness of life in general.

This attitude is broken by the crashing chord which unites Buddha and St. Augustine, and we have Eliot's note that 'the collocation of these two representations of Eastern and Western asceticism as the culmination of this part of the poem, is not an accident.' Both the great religious teachers see the destructive elements in life in terms of fire. The broken prayer of the protagonist that he may be a brand plucked from the burning, leads on naturally to the next section, the possibility of the purification.

The 'Death by Water,' however, is no simple surrender into hope of rebirth through baptism. The Sibyl's words 'I wish to die' are an undercurrent all through. The whole rhythm indeed, the quiet, drifting peace of it, suggest the pull towards final forgetfulness. Yet the fact that its central figure is a composite of the Phoenician sailor and the merchant points in the other direction. They are symbols of the initiates of the mystery religions, going back to the fertility cults with their ritual of consigning the effigy of the god to the sea and welcoming it as reborn at the end of its journey, carried by a predictable current. On this level it symbolizes the relinquishing of 'the natural man' to 'the current under sea'; to the metamorphosis suggested by 'picked his bones in whispers,' which seems to suggest both the disintegration of the old life, and the mystery and half-heard message of the new. It recalls

Ariel's 'of his bones are coral made' and 'the wild waves whist.' It means 'entering the whirlpool,' a moment of terrifying surrender, but also the peace of becoming 'free from attachment' in Buddha's words; from the attachments of the sense world, 'the cry of gulls, and the deep sea swell'; from the preoccupation of charting an individual course; from the measurement of the importance of life in terms of 'age and youth' and of personal attraction:

> O you who turn the wheel and look to windward,
> Consider Phlebas, who was once handsome and tall as you.

The poem is addressed to 'Gentile or Jew,' which sends us to the chapters in the Epistle to the Romans where Paul argues that the new life in Christ belongs equally to both. He insists too on the inseparability of life and death in the regeneration: 'so many of us as were baptized into Jesus Christ were baptized into his death. Therefore we are buried with him by baptism into death.' [9]

This memory forms the transition to the opening of the next and last section of the poem, where there is no peace. The knight may have taken the decision to set out on his quest, the initiate to submit to his trials, but the outcome is all uncertain, the ordeals only too present. In this part of the poem there are no actors in the contemporary Waste Land. The drama has become purely an inward one of tortured personal consciousness, flung back and forth between hope and despair, haunted by landscapes of horror, lit only by a flash of lightning, refreshed only by the 'damp gust bringing rain.' But the poem does not end with the coming of rain. The Chapel Perilous is reached, but what happens afterwards is ambiguous,

[9] Romans VI 3-4.

and at the end the Fisher King, though the arid plain is *behind* him, is still fishing, still questioning if any achievement is ahead.

St. Paul's linking of baptism and death is the starting point, the biblical scenes evoked in a sequence of powerful sense-images. And the Christian mystery of life through death is linked with the vegetation myths in their great common thundering rhythm of hope and resurrection. But the conclusion of the opening passage may mean either of two things, or both.

> He who was living is now dead
> We who were living are now dying
> With a little patience

That is, Tammuz, Adonis, Osiris, Dionysus, Christ, are no longer alive in the modern world. Mankind, whose life was fertilized and enriched through these symbolic concepts, no longer responds to them, 'feeding a little life with dried tubers.' But it may be a reference to the time between the death of the god and his resurrection—the time he spends in the underworld—or, for the disciple, the period of initiation, with the combined waiting and suffering which 'patience' implies. Certainly the protagonist is on his way to the Chapel Perilous, and his journey is through a drought more parching and agonizing than anything experienced before in the poem. The peace of 'Death by Water' seems utterly negated. There is not only no water and no sound of water, but there is not even silence. He is tortured by 'dry sterile thunder without rain,' and there is not even solitude; hostile figures 'sneer and snarl' at his endeavour, as he struggles up the sandy road or has the nightmare sense of constriction in a cave:

> Dead mountain mouth of carious teeth that cannot spit
> Here one can neither stand nor lie nor sit

There is only the vision, which may be a desert mirage, of the hooded figure of the risen god who accompanied the disciples to Emmaus.

This is but a glimpsed possibility, however, followed by what Eliot tells us is the theme of 'the present decay of Eastern Europe'—the birthplace of all the religions of the ancient world. The quotation from Hermann Hesse in the notes says that already at least half of Eastern Europe is on the way to chaos. It goes along singing drunkenly in spiritual madness. The bourgeois laughs at these songs, the saint and seer hear them with tears. Eliot, giving the scenes the setting of the violet light of the twilight of civilization, and the 'maternal lamentations' of these lands that mothered ancient glories, creates a chaos of destruction and nightmare distortions of sight and sound. It is all 'Unreal,' partly because of the indeterminate 'hooded hordes' and the outlines of the city; partly because of the phantasmagoria of horror which the vision brings; the sight of the falling cities, of the woman fiddling on her hair, of the bats with baby faces crawling down the walls. To this is added the medley of sounds: the 'whisper music,' so different from the whispers in 'Death by Water'; the whistling bats beating their wings; the reminiscent bells, tolling from the towers—the symbols of aspiration—now 'upside down in air,' no longer created on human ground; and the echoing voices singing from the empty cisterns and wells that once held the living waters of faith.

But though these may be suggestions of the nightmare of contemporary civilization, they are also parallels of the ghosts and ghouls which haunted the Chapel and Cemetery Perilous in the Grail romance, and Miss Weston sees these as all relics of the initiation ceremonies into the mystery cults concerned with the attainment of increased spiritual powers. They link with all the myths dealing with journeys to the nether world, and are all, according to Jung, different archetypal images of the same psychological process. There is always the danger that the psyche may not return to the world of men, but may perish in the desert of drought or pass permanently into the realms of phantasmagoria. The chapel here is surrounded by the graves and dry bones of those who have failed in the quest, and it is itself an empty shell, 'only the wind's home.' One of the most painful ordeals of the knights, Miss Weston tells us, was the suggestion that the chapel itself was a delusion, and here it seems at first to be part of the same empty lifelessness of the towers and cisterns and exhausted wells. But it is not 'reminiscent bells' that continue to toll, but the living bird that salutes the dawn and drives evil spirits to their lairs.

The cock-crow heralds 'a damp gust, bringing rain,' but instead of experiencing the rain, we pass to the parable of the thunder, an Indian myth from the Upanishads. This is not the 'dry, sterile thunder,' but the voice of the supreme Lord of Creation, answering the request of his offspring that he should speak to them. Thus it is another version of the 'question' which runs through the poem. The answers are accepted by the protagonist as the way of active endeavour which will bring peace, but his own response is equivocal and wavering. In a passage of stirring rhythmical assurance and a mingling of seventeenth century dramatic echoes with his own powerful verse movement, he announces his entering of the 'whirlpool'; the assertion of the 'real,' the act of life, an act outside the life and death cycle in the temporal pattern.

> What have we given?
> My friend, blood shaking my heart
> The awful daring of a moment's surrender
> Which an age of prudence can never retract
> By this, and this only, we have existed
> Which is not to be found in our obituaries
> Or in memories draped by the beneficent spider
> Or under seals broken by the lean solicitor
> In our empty rooms.

But the surrender, though it is an irrevocable commitment, is partial only. In consequence, the second demand, 'sympathize,' brings little hope. After that 'moment's surrender,' he has heard the key turn in his prison, just as Ugolino did in his hunger tower. He has heard no sound of the door being *un*-locked. He is still in the prison of negative isolation, the condition described by Bradley as 'a circle closed on the out-side.' It is the condition of the broken Coriolanus, broken because he was unable to keep faith with a central loyalty outside himself. It is in dreams only, and fleeting ones at that, that he can recapture the sense of freedom from imprisonment. Such an 'aethereal rumour' of release is the next fragment, with its beautiful flowing rhythm: the vision of a boat on a calm sea in the control of skilled hands. Had he been able to make the surrender complete that would have been the image of his own heart.

The longed-for release from sterility, the resolution of the conflict in the opening lines of Part 1, has not come. 'Shall I at least set my lands in order?' asks the Fisher King: can he at least try to rebuild *his* 'ruins,' to abnegate the attitude of passive negation, to *do* something more than sit fishing while 'London Bridge is falling down falling down falling down.' Then follows a series of quotations, which he says are 'frag-ments I have shored against my ruins.' They are fragments like the 'heap of broken images' and the 'withered stumps of time' in the rest of the poem. They tell of all that he longs for and feels unable to achieve. But instead of merely lamenting the loss of their reality in the whole waste land of the present he sets himself to bring them into relation with *his* lands and *his* ruins. Each picks up the theme of rebirth woven through the whole texture of the poem, but instead of the attitude of disgust towards the 'dirty ears' which can no longer hear that message, in each fragment a poet speaks of the theme in rela-tion to his own personal emotional state. The first is Arnaut Daniel, the Provençal poet Dante meets in Purgatory. He tells how he is suffering for his lustful life on earth, but how he welcomes his pain, he sings as he weeps, because of his hope of final redemption. 'Then he dived back into that fire which refines them.' Next is a line from the *Pervigilium Veneris*. It is a song of spring and fulfilment. The nightingale sings, her cruel memories forgotten, and the poet alone is sad and silent. 'When will spring awaken in me?' he cries, 'When shall I be as the swallow, that I may cease to be voiceless?' Procne, Philomela's sister, was changed to a swallow as a rebirth from her sufferings, and the connection is emphasized by Eliot in a note. The third line is from a sonnet by Gerard de Nerval, *The Disinherited One*. The poet, bereft and inconsolable, like 'the Prince of Aquitaine at the ruined tower,' has lost all, but he resolves to reclaim and rebuild his heritage.

These then are, as it were, memories which may help him to 'order' his own lands, they give hopes of roots that may clutch and branches that may grow out of his 'stony rubbish.' But at the same time there *is* no image of renewed life in himself in this conclusion. Fragments shored against ruins bring no sense of organic union and renewed life. And the next quotation perhaps points to this, though it is very obscure and my interpretation is pure guesswork. Cleanth Brooks' comment on it is this:

> 'The protagonist's acceptance of what is in reality the deepest truth will seem to the present world mere madness. ('And still she cried, and still the world pursues,/"Jug Jug" to dirty ears.') Hieronymo in the play, like Hamlet, was 'mad' for a purpose. The protagonist is conscious of the interpretation which will be placed on the words which follow—words which will seem to many apparently meaningless babble, but which contain the oldest and most permanent truth of the race: *Datta. Dayadhvam. Damyata.*'

But this is not very convincing. For one thing it ignores the words 'Why then Ile fit you.' Hieronymo in the play has been

asked to provide a 'show' for the entertainment of the king.
He replies with these words, and says he has a tragedy he wrote
in his youth. He plans to use this, fitting the actors to the
parts he wants them to play in a drama of real life. Moreover
there is another strange aspect of this play:

> Each one of us must act his part
> In unknown languages . . .

He is not pretending to be mad at all in this scene, and the
second half of the line, 'Hieronymo's mad againe' stands by
itself and is not, I think, in *The Spanish Tragedy,* but is an
invention of Eliot's. Hieronymo's trouble, like Hamlet's, is that
he procrastinates and cannot take action. The times when he
is really mad with grief are those when he ceases to argue about
action, and so he says:

> I am never better than when I am mad;
> Then methinks I am a brave fellow
> Then I do wonders, but reason abuseth me;
> And there's the torment, there's the hell.

May there have been an association of all these 'fragments' in
Eliot's mind? He is casting himself, 'fitting' himself in the
parts, 'in sundry languages' of these other poets who have
suffered and struggled to achieve new life. It is when he is
'mad,' when he remembers 'the awful daring of a moment's
surrender,' that he feels able to say the concluding words of
the poem:

> Datta. Dayadhvam. Damyata.
> Shantih shantih shantih

Eliot's note on the conclusion is: 'Shantih. Repeated as
here, a formal ending to an Upanishad. "The Peace which
passeth understanding" is our equivalent to this word.' But it
is impossible to feel peace in the concluding passage. It is a

formal ending only. The atmosphere is coloured far more strongly by the image of destruction 'London Bridge is falling down falling down falling down,' and by the sense of attempting to shore up the ruins by repeating words of comfort and strengthening of the spirit which may help him. But they are in foreign tongues, not translated into his own inner experience and so become a part of himself. *Give, Sympathize, Control, Peace,* remain abstract ideas; none of them has been transfigured into a redeeming symbol. The surrender has been made, but it still seems a surrender to death, and the possibility of rebirth is still without substance or outline.

CHAPTER VI

❖◆❖

The Hollow Men

Those of us who find ourselves supporting what Mr.
Murry calls Classicism believe that men cannot get on
without giving allegiance to something outside themselves. I am aware that 'outside' and 'inside' are terms
which provide unlimited opportunity for quibbling, and
that no psychologist would tolerate a discussion which
shuffled such base coinage; but I will presume that Mr.
Murry and myself can agree that for our purpose these
counters are adequate, and concur in disregarding the
admonitions of our psychological friends. If you find that
you have to imagine it as outside, then it is outside.

T. S. ELIOT. *The Function of Criticism*

FROM a letter Pound wrote to Eliot early in 1922,[1] we
know that Conrad's *Heart of Darkness* was very much
in his mind at the time he wrote *The Waste Land*. He
contemplated using the quotation 'Mistah Kurtz—he dead' as
the epigraph, and was persuaded by Pound that it was not
substantial enough to sustain that position. The only direct
influence of the Conrad story is in the first of the songs of the
Thames-daughters in Part III. *Heart of Darkness* opens with
a very fine description of the Pool of London, and in the course
of it Conrad writes: 'Nothing is easier . . . than to evoke the
great spirit of the past upon the lower reaches of the Thames.'
The detail of 'the tanned sails of the barges drifting up with
the tide seemed to stand still in red clusters of canvas,' is
echoed in

[1] Eliot House Collection. Harvard.

The barges drift
With the turning tide
Red sails
Wide
To leeward . . .

But the story itself, with its haunting creation of the lost soul who had obviously passed through the initiation into some savage mystery cult and had been broken by the experience, is not in any way evoked. Nor indeed is it in *The Hollow Men,* but the epigraph turns our attention to the story, and a study of it brings out some interesting parallels between some of the comments of Marlowe, who tells it, and attitudes which appear in the poem, and which we may perhaps attribute to Eliot at this time.

Psychologically, the experience in *The Hollow Men* is even more despairing than that of the conclusion of *The Waste Land*. The full horror of the situation of spiritual stagnation is experienced, without the actively dramatized revulsion from the contemporary scene, or the actively dramatized inner struggle between compulsion and revulsion towards personal change. The poet sees himself inescapably identified with his environment, and any power of choice or movement towards action of any sort seems utterly paralyzed. It is a condition which Jung, as well as Eliot, characterizes symbolically as the meeting with the Shadow. To Jung it is the confronting of our own inner 'darkness,' which means 'bitter shock, though it is the indispensable prerequisite of every renewal of the spirit.' The 'death by water' will appear first as a real spiritual death; the surrender seems to lead to 'a boundless expanse full of unprecedented uncertainty, with apparently no inside and no outside, no above and no below, no here and no there, no mine and no thine, no good and no bad.' [2] And this is the dangerous moment, 'in which the decision takes place between annihilation and new life.'

[2] *Integration of the Personality,* p. 70.

The essential prelude to any new life is the appearance of a new redeeming symbol from the unconscious which shall be a new centre of energy, the focus of fresh effort. No such symbol appeared in *The Waste Land:* the cock-crow brought no glad dawn, the damp gust no saving shower. The final picture is of the lonely fisher with the arid plain behind him. All he can do is to recall 'the awful daring' of the moment of surrender, to remind himself of others who have succeeded in the quest, and pronounce the *words* at least of the saving formula. In *The Hollow Men* what the poet feels to be the redeeming symbol has appeared, but only to be lost again: hence the despair created in the poem. The faint heartbeat of the rhythm throughout, the recurrent images of deadness of sensibility, and the abstract vocabulary into which the poem finally passes embody a sense of psychic depletion far more spectral than the violent emotional conflict in *The Waste Land*. Any hope that the 'eyes' may reappear is negated by the despairing acceptance of defeat, by the compulsion to *avoid* any further struggle; by the final failure even to continue to formulate positive and negative positions, and the resulting collapse into the whimpering announcement of annihilation.

The dramatic oppositions too are no longer between symbols of a vital past and a dying present, or between creative and destructive attitudes towards experience. They are between different qualities of self-destruction—between Mr. Kurtz and Guy Fawkes on the one hand, and the hollow men, among which the poet himself is numbered. He can no longer project his own 'darkness' upon all the elements in his environment to which he feels alien, but superior. He can no longer find any release in the exposure of the hollowness and horror of a Sweeney, of a decadent 'landlord,' of a Madame Sosostris, of empty, aimless women and young men carbuncular. He himself is a dweller in darkness as deep as that of those he had so surely and cynically displayed, and far deeper than that of those 'lost violent souls' in history or imaginative creation, who, if damned, were at least damned for overt action, and not for the condition of

> Shape without form, shade without colour,
> Paralyzed force, gesture without motion.

The self-destruction by *deeds*, even if evil, is preferable to passive non-entity. 'So far as we are human, what we do must be either evil or good; so far as we do evil or good, we are human; and it is better, in a paradoxical way, to do evil than to do nothing: at least, we exist.'[3] The real Guy Fawkes, whose memory is now reduced to the light-hearted burning of him in effigy, to dances around a bonfire, and the begging of pennies for fireworks, at least had the courage of his convictions. Waiting in his gunpowder-filled 'dry cellar,' he was willing to face death in the 'bang' of an explosion of the House of Commons. Even Mr. Kurtz, who had succumbed to African 'black magic,' goes to death 'with direct eyes,' with a 'wide and immense stare embracing, condemning, loathing all the universe,' whispering his final summing up of human experience: 'The horror! The horror!' Marlowe, confronted with the 'choice of nightmares,' the choice between taking the side of Kurtz or that of the 'mean and greedy phantoms' of the purely commercial interests, unhesitatingly chooses loyalty to Kurtz. His terrible last words seem to him 'the expression of some form of belief . . . it had the appalling face of a glimpsed truth. It was an affirmation, a moral victory paid for by innumerable defeats, by abominable terrors, by abominable satisfactions. But it was a victory!'[4]

Marlowe himself, the imaginative rationalist, owns that when he himself faced death, it was in a 'sickly atmosphere of tepid skepticism,' a 'vision of greyness without form,' and that

---

[3] *Baudelaire*, Selected Essays, p. 377.
[4] *Youth and Two Other Stories.* Joseph Conrad. Doubleday, Page & Co., N. Y., 1916, p. 172.

he found with humiliation that he 'had nothing to say.' He returns to Paris and to a mood when he moves through 'the sepulchral city' as through 'some inconceivable world that had no hope in it and no desire.' Finally he takes the packet of letters intrusted to him, to Kurtz's 'Intended,' and in her he finds an 'inextinguishable light of belief and love,' based on the illusion that Kurtz had remained true to the end to her and to his early ideals. 'Her dark eyes looked out at me. Their glance was guileless, profound, confident and trustful.' Naturally, Marlowe refuses to quench that faith and to let in 'the triumphant darkness.' He tells her nothing of the truth. 'By the last gleams of twilight I could see the glitter of her eyes, full of tears—of tears that would not fall.'

But the symbol of the eyes in *The Hollow Men,* which are the only hope of overcoming the Shadow, cannot belong to any vision of romantic illusion, any more than they can be Kurtz's 'wide and immense stare.' In Part I they are the 'direct eyes' of those of assured faith, who have died, but later the symbol absorbs much richer implications. The opening of Part II is somewhat ambiguous, as it is difficult to know whether the 'there' in the fourth line refers to 'in dreams' or to 'in death's dream kingdom' (which is the death-in-life of the world of the hollow men). I read it that the poet dare not meet the direct eyes in dreams, for they light his ruins, reveal the lovely freedom of wind and tree and arouse poetic and spiritual memories 'distant and solemn,' in place of the 'quiet and meaningless' voices of the opening lines. His world is a dying planet, doomed to extinction, and he prays to be left in it, a stuffed effigy, a scarecrow, 'behaving as the wind behaves,' that is, acted *upon*, not acting, having no responsibility for his own fate. With terror he recoils from coming face to face with the eyes, from

> that final meeting
> In the twilight kingdom

when, in the purgatory of active spiritual regeneration he, like Dante, would see the severe eyes of Beatrice directed upon him, and hear her stern words of reproach.[5]

Parts III and IV develop the horror of 'death's dream kingdom.' The images of the dryness, the nullity, the emptiness are joined by further symbols of agonizing frustration. Both the worshipper and the thing worshipped are equally lifeless:

> Here the stone images
> Are raised, here they receive
> The supplication of a dead man's hand

Faith can give nothing to satisfy the passionate desire for warm human comfort and communion, and he asks if death itself, 'death's other kingdom' would mean the same thing.

The water symbol here has no regenerative value. It is the 'tumid river' as described in *Heart of Darkness:* 'this stillness of life did not in the least resemble a peace . . . An empty stream, a great silence.' Life is nothing but 'this broken jaw of our lost kingdoms'—a packed image which suggests the deadness and dryness of existence, its incapacity for articulation and communication and its isolation from a body within which it could function as a living member. It also suggests the whole concept that such entity as this life has bears only as much relation to the whole 'kingdom' of man's estate, as the single bone from which a zoologist guesses at the whole living organism that once existed.

After this torturing picture of hollowness, loneliness, darkness and deadness, we are reminded again of Dante and Beatrice; of how, after his repentance, she bathed him in the river of Lethe, and her stern gaze turned to smiling encouragement, to 'eyes of light.' Of how she conducted him upwards and he saw the Divine Essence as an intensely shining Point, 'and like a star in heaven the truth was seen'; and of how

---

[5] *Purgatorio.* Canto XXX.

finally he saw Paradise as a 'multifoliate rose' of saints, the
crown and consummation of that willing condemnation to the
spiritual purgatory of 'death's twilight kingdom.' But the conclusion again is ambiguous.

> The hope only
> Of empty men

may mean that even the hollow men hope for such a revelation,
or, more probably, that it is only empty men who put their
hopes so high, omitting any action towards climbing the mount
of purgatory which must precede it.

There is certainly no hope in the conclusion. Instead of any
vision, any release, any forward movement, any light or any
'wind's singing,' there is the eternal going *round* in the cactus
land, enclosed in time and place, in a childish nursery-rhyme
world of make-believe. Then, passing out of the concrete
evocation of physical parallels, the poet conceives of the
Shadow as 'paralyzed force,' as that abstract principle of the
negation of the will, which either uses the forms of prayer without the substance of action, or evades the issue by a post-
ponement: 'Life is very long.' Finally, the Shadow triumphs,
not in any vision of cataclysmic violence, as at the conclusion
of *Gerontion,* but from sheer inanition of the spirit to make
any affirmative response. The only possible step from the
'essence' of the poet's present despair, enclosed in his 'dry
cellar,' would be the active 'descent,' the repudiation of his
faint dream visions of empty hope, the entrance into the
'twilight kingdom.' But he is lost in the Shadow, and his 'world
ends' not in any self-chosen dark night of the soul, but in a
sense of tormented, whimpering vacuity.

CHAPTER VII

❖❖❖

Ash Wednesday

> Love has her priests in the poets, and sometimes you
> will hear a voice which knows how to hold her in honour:
> but not a word will you hear about faith. Who is there
> who can speak in honour of this passion?
>
> S. KIERKEGAARD. *Fear and Trembling*

ELIOT has said that there are essentially two ways in
which poetry can add to human experience. One is by
perceiving and recording the world of sense and feeling at any given moment; the other by extending the frontiers
of that world into a wider and loftier one. It is Dante above
all who thus extends the frontiers of actuality, and Eliot in
his own way has done the same thing. Although no poetry
could be more concrete in detail, image and scenery, all are
part of an inner world, a visionary and symbolic landscape.
In *Ash Wednesday* this landscape changes its character. Some
of the old symbols remain, but their emotional quality is
subtly changed and shifted by the appearance of new ones
which combine with them. The new dominating figure is that of
a Lady, but inseparable from her is a garden, a rose, a fountain and two yew trees. These all form a new symbolic *centre,*
in which the poet finds a renewal of life. They alternate with a
desert of sand and of blue rocks, and there are further contrasting images of sounds and silence; of movement and stillness; of disintegration and reintegration; of light and darkness;
of loneliness and companionship. The fragments of liturgy
appearing in most of the separate poems also take on the
character of a symbol; and the whole is controlled by images

of *transition*, of 'turning' from one condition to another, and in the third part, of climbing a circular stair. It is obvious that the whole poem is coloured by religious and literary tradition, but its particular quality is entirely its own.

In *Ash Wednesday*, what Jung calls the 'dangerous moment,' the hovering between the possibility of permanent distortion or of the total arrest of growth on the one hand, and the possibility of fertility springing from spiritual renewal on the other, is over. That was present throughout *The Waste Land*, but was at its greatest intensity in *The Hollow Men*. There, 'unless the eyes reappear,' the spirit seems doomed to permanent imprisonment in the 'dry cellar' of the ego. But in *Ash Wednesday* that danger is past. This does not mean any assured position of safety and security, but it means that the new redeeming symbols are established as the new centre from which the new life will radiate and in which it has its being. It is to pass from dwelling wholly in 'death's dream kingdom' to the 'dream-crossed twilight' of a new world; to feel, at least intermittently, the capacity to experience *reality, act, creation, response, spasm, existence.* Instead of the sense of complete exhaustion and defeat, there is one of a gradual spiritual clarification, of process and progress, though within that, there is still both progression and regression, 'a rhythm of destruction and construction, of error and truth, of loss and gain, of depth and height.' [1]

The emotional condition may seem little different from that in *The Hollow Men*, but the *attitude* toward the condition is changed completely. The complete passivity of the opening poem has nothing in it of negative frustration. In place of hopeless abandonment to the blighting power of the Shadow, the compulsion to evade and escape, there is the *willed* renunciation and patience of a *chosen* attitude. Jung describes this as a condition of 'not doing,' which is quite different from that of 'doing nothing'; a condition through which the new forces

[1] Jung. *Integration of the Personality*, p. 89.

alive in the new symbols gain strength by allowing them possession; by becoming object not subject. The symbols themselves dramatize the inner conflict, while the conscious will collaborates by its own disciplines. In Eliot's poem this is represented forcibly by the reminders of traditional worship to which the poet turns perpetually in his distress. The individual vision of his personal redeeming symbols comes and goes, but prayer is a technique of concentration to which he reverts throughout. The poem returns again and again to it; to the submission of the penitent, to the *ordering* power of a discipline, to the placing of the individual within the traditional corporate experience of the race. At the same time it is a poem of intensely personal emotion, though it is removed from anything like romantic subjectivism by the interposing of the symbolic emblems, and by the distancing of the whole experience into its own esthetic world.

Of the particular qualities of this world Eliot himself has given a description in his essay on Dante. Commenting there on the similarities between the *Vita Nuova,* and *The Shepherd of Hermas* of the second century, he says: 'The similarities might prove that a certain *habit* of dream imagery can persist throughout many changes of civilization . . . I suggest that possibly Dante, in his place and time, was following something more essential than merely a "literary" tradition.' Eliot defines the general medieval practice of allegorizing experience as the ordering of it into 'clear visual imagery,' which sprang from the quality of thinking in an age when men still saw visions. 'We have nothing but dreams, and we have forgotten that seeing visions . . . was once a more significant, interesting and disciplined kind of dreaming.' The work of Dante, he says, 'belongs to the world of what I call the *high dream,* and the modern world seems capable only of the low dream.'

Ash Wednesday certainly belongs to the world of high

dream, and its reminiscences of the world of Dante have been pointed out frequently. More particularly the figure of the Lady inevitably recalls that of Beatrice. Eliot's own remarks on the *Vita Nuova* suggest strongly that he sees in the story of the relationship of Dante to Beatrice a mixture of the personal and the imaginative which parallels something in his own life, something which also had its root in a childhood memory. He sees it as a fundamental human experience which can be understood only 'by accustoming ourselves to find meaning in *final causes* rather than in origins.' The origins may appear physical and sexual, but 'the final cause is attraction towards God.' Again, when distinguishing between 'romantic' and 'classical' mysticism, Eliot declares that it is characteristic of romantic mysticism to *substitute* divine love for human love, whereas in Dante the effort was to enlarge the boundary of human love so as to make it a stage in the progress toward the divine. It was a method of utilizing, transforming instead of discarding, the emotions of adolescence, whereby the area of the emotion was extended, through the expression of love as contemplation of the beauty and goodness of the beloved object. He regards the experience which forms the material of the *Vita Nuova* as the material of adolescence, but handled by a mature man with the philosophy which assigns a place to such experience.

He concludes that the *Vita Nuova,* besides being an example of 'vision literature' is 'a very sound psychological treatise on something related to what is now called "sublimation." ' In this Jung would certainly concur, and would interpret both Beatrice and the Lady as examples of the *anima* archetype, the woman image which, according to his theory, regularly appears at this stage in the process of 'transformation.' The *anima,* in spite of its name, is in no sense a 'soul' image in the religious sense. It is the 'contra-sexual component' alive in every man, and its images, like the other archetypes, have both creative and destructive aspects. In itself it is a primitive and compulsive force, which, when it has no 'ordering' function, may be created in man's myth-making imagination as Venus, or Helen of Troy, as Morgan le Fay or La Belle Dame sans Merci. 'An element of the supernatural always adheres to the anima. This must be so, since she is an entity living almost entirely in the "other world" of the unconscious.' But as a symbol in the process of spiritual regeneration, the figure always appears to hold 'something like a secret intention, which seems to spring from a superior knowledge of the laws of life . . . and the more this meaning is recognized, the more does the anima lose its impetuous, impulsive and compulsive character.'[2] It becomes instead the symbol of hidden wisdom, the 'enlightener,' the *mediating* function between the conscious ego and the inner world of the unconscious. It is the 'enabling' power, though at the same time it remains mysterious and ambiguous, 'a complexly opalescent phenomenon.'

The poem as a whole has much that is mysterious and ambiguous in it, in spite of several elucidations,[3] and we cannot hope to find any easy allegorical content of the various symbols. They remain 'complexly opalescent,' as do the constantly shifting moods and tones. And just as it takes us into a new world of psychic experience, so is its rhythmical organization, imagery and language unlike any earlier poem of Eliot. It swings with the 'turning world' of the poet's inner consciousness, while it is framed and controlled by the unchanging ritual of common prayer.

It has been pointed out[4] that the condition in the opening poem is that of the initiate who enters the 'dark night' of St. John of the Cross. He must achieve 'a spiritual detachment from all things, whether sensual or spiritual, and a leaning on

[2] *Integration of the Personality,* p. 80.
[3] Leonard Unger in *T. S. Eliot. A Selected Critique.* E. E. Duncan Jones in *T. S. Eliot. A Study of His Writings by Several Hands.*
[4] By Leonard Unger.

pure faith alone.' There is a quiet acceptance of temporary exile from hope and a refusal to admit despair in its place. Instead, the act of renunciation itself can be made a cause for rejoicing, since it is a willed act, an annunciation in positive terms of submission to the 'negative way.' When we know that the first line is a translation from a farewell ballad of Guido Cavalcanti to his 'lady,' describing his afflictions dying in exile from her, it adds much to its force. The inner interplay of 'turn' and 'return' comes in from the start, and the sense of exile from a loved figure as well as from 'the usual reign.' The poet has put aside all 'striving'; all the mood of Shakespeare's sonnet [5] where, weeping his outcast state, he curses his fate,

> Wishing me like to one more rich in hope . . .
> Desiring this man's art and that man's scope.

Shakespeare finds release in thinking of his love:

> and then my state,
> Like to the lark at break of day arising
> From sullen earth, sings hymns at heaven's gate;
> For thy sweet love remembered such wealth brings
> That then I scorn to change my state with kings.

But this kind of happy change from frustration to fulfilment has no place in Eliot's mood. In a parenthesis he suggests '(Why should the agèd eagle stretch its wings?)' where the sensation matches the *striving* of the line before, and there is an implied contrast to Shakespeare's lark. The image has been related [6] to a medieval legend that the eagle in old age flies up to the sun, where his feathers are burnt off and he falls into a fountain of water whence he issues with his youth renewed. In this way it is a symbol of spiritual regeneration. In the context Eliot seems to be suggesting simply 'Why identify one-

[5] No. XXIX.
[6] By E. E. Duncan Jones.

self with any regal image of dramatic renewal?' The renunciation of 'striving' involves the renunciation of all that order of
'state'; the kingdom, the power and the glory of the 'usual
reign.'

But the second verse implies the further renunciation of
spiritual as well as material power and glory. In the love-code
of the Provençal lyric poets, their 'lady' represented an object
outside possessive sexual love. While she was worshipped as a
human being, she was contemplated also as the source of aspiration and inspiration on the highest spiritual level. Cavalcanti is bidding farewell to that too, and here it is the hope of
the return of such spiritual strength, as well as the hope of
temporal and 'actual' joys that the poet puts behind him. He
renounces 'the infirm glory of the positive hour,' but also 'the
one veritable transitory power,' the one thing 'in this brief
transit where the dreams cross' (Part vi), which gives him a
sense of *relationship* between this world and some firm glory
beyond it. This is the Lady herself, 'the blessèd face and voice,'
and the garden and the fountain, 'there, where trees flower and
springs flow.' Instead of the vision of the Lady and the power
to drink from her symbolic fount of life, 'there is nothing
again,' and he turns to make something of that nothing, turns
from the contemplation of ends to that of means. Cause and
consequence seem paradoxical when the renunciation of hope
can bring rejoicing, but it is in faith and penitence alone that
such an attitude can be sustained, and the broken rhythms of
the opening become firm and affirmative as they assert that
attitude. Instead of the endless torturing turnings of self-
debate,

> These matters that with myself I too much discuss
> Too much explain

he submits himself in prayer to the mercy and judgment of
God.

The wings of his spirit are neither those of the agèd eagle

nor those of the lark singing at heaven's gate, but nevertheless they do not drop or droop. They 'beat the air'; they have a winnowing function, and their action suggests too his own chosen condition of *active* patience in the small dry air of complete deprivation. His will at least need not capitulate and accept the resignation of despair. It is the distinction between 'not doing' and 'doing nothing'; it is both caring and not caring.

The conclusion in the words from the *Ave Maria* merge the individual consciousness into the collective response represented by ritual. The words of the familiar invocation both blend and contrast with the emotive power of his own lines. They also replace his own lost vision of 'the blessèd face and voice' with thoughts of the supreme mediating 'Lady' of the Church.

In his essay on Pascal Eliot says:

> It is a commonplace that some forms of illness are extremely favourable, not only to religious illumination, but to artistic and literary composition. A piece of writing meditated, apparently without progress, for months or years, may suddenly take shape and word; and in this state long passages may be produced which require little or no retouch . . . he to whom this happens assuredly has the sensation of being a vehicle rather than a maker.

I have no means of knowing if the second poem of *Ash Wednesday* was composed in this way, but it is certainly one of the passages in Eliot which *reads* as if it had come without conscious effort. There is a feeling of exhausted vitality in the first poem, where the conscious will is labouring to 'construct' an advance on the principle of causation and consequence, and the wings of the spirit are 'merely vans to beat the air.' Prayer, the concentration on the traditional ritual of mediation, is the only activity, and it is carried on in an atmosphere of shrinkage

and constriction which, however gladly accepted, is by definition the deprivation of both sense and spirit. In the second
poem, however, the rejoicing in the situation is no longer a
matter of a discipline of renunciation. It has translated itself
into the spontaneity of vision, into joyous, grotesque and beautiful symbols. The desert of *The Waste Land* is seen in a new
light. There the disintegration of the personality was

> A heap of broken images, where the sun beats,
> And the dead tree gives no shelter, the cricket no relief,
> And the dry stone no sound of water.

But here the whole emotional colouring is changed. The bones
are not 'stony rubbish' or those later 'rattled by the rat's feet';
the dead tree is a live juniper; the beating sun has given place
to 'the cool of the day'; the negative 'no sound of water' to the
positive 'quiet.' The cricket which brings no relief has become
the chirping grasshopper; the red rock of the subsequent lines
has dissolved into the radiant whiteness and brightness which
lights the whole poem, (the liturgical colour of faith and joy);
and 'fear in a handful of dust' is thereby transformed into 'the
blessing of sand' and the happy bones 'glad to be scattered.'
For the scattering of the bones is the symbol of the dissolution
of the old ego as the centre of being, while the Rose and the
Garden become the new centre. 'Belladonna, the Lady of the
Rocks/The lady of situations' has been transformed into this
gracious reconciling figure through whom the poet reaches his
revelation, and to whom, therefore, the bones address their
song. The song itself has none of the formality of a traditional
litany, but is a fresh and personal creation of the central
symbolism.

The specific reference is to the thirty-seventh chapter of
Ezekiel, the vision of 'the valley which was full of bones,' and
to this is added an association from 1 Kings XIX. When
Elijah fled from Jezebel, 'He went a day's journey into the
wilderness, and came and sat down under a juniper tree: and

he requested for himself that he might die.' And when Ezekiel went to the valley of the bones: 'There were very many in the open valley, and lo, they were very dry. And he said unto me, Son of man, can these bones live? . . . Again he said unto me, Prophesy upon these bones and say unto them . . . I will cause breath to enter into you, and ye shall live . . . Prophesy unto the wind . . . So I prophesied as he commanded and the breath came into them, and they lived.'

The three white leopards have puzzled commentators, but perhaps Eliot did have a dream in which he saw them! They are in the tradition of all the *devouring* myths in which the hero is swallowed and emerges regenerated, just as the scattering of the bones tells of the same psychic reality as the dismemberment of Dionysus or of Osiris. The leopards are devouring beasts, but obviously at the same time beneficent ones. Their whiteness and their quiet pose show them to be harmless: they lose terror in beauty. Moreover, as the bones know very well, the loss of the parts devoured by the leopards has made it possible for the brightness of the Lady to shine upon them. The ego which has been dispersed gladly relinquishes itself:

> And I who am here dissembled
> Proffer my deeds to oblivion, and my love
> To the posterity of the desert and the fruit of the gourd.

In these enchanting and chant-like lines, the body, whose old likeness has been changed and scattered (dissembled), renounces its past and the sensual aspects of its love. And having made the renunciation, it finds that the loss is not complete dismemberment. It is a losing and forgetting of the old, followed by a 'recovery' through which something new can come into being. The earlier emotions are not discarded, but utilized and transformed, and the area of emotion extended by centring love in contemplation of the beauty and goodness of the beloved object: 'Thus devoted, concentrated in purpose,' the wind of the spirit may come.

The reference to Ecclesiastes in the last line 'and the grass-hopper shall be a burden, and desire shall fail: because man goeth to his long home,' is another detail in which the scene differs from its parallel in *The Waste Land*. It is the poem which the bones 'chirp' which is the 'burden' (the refrain of a song), and the 'desire' which has failed is not a prelude to death, but to a new aspect of love.

The 'burden,' with the mingled biblical and medieval flavour of the word, takes us into a new atmosphere in a litany to the Lady, who is herself withdrawn 'in a white gown, to contemplation, in a white gown.' The Garden is a many-faceted symbol, suggesting the Garden of Eden where God walked 'in the cool of the day'; the earthly Paradise of Dante; the rose-garden of the *Romance of the Rose;* and medieval hymns to the Virgin which allegorize the rose and the 'garden enclosed' of the *Song of Songs* as the womb of Mary. At the opening of the lyric, however, the Lady is the mediating figure between the two sequences of love, carnal and spiritual, and therefore subsumes both:

> Calm and distressed
> Torn and most whole . . .
> Exhausted and life-giving
> Worried reposeful

She is the rose of memory and forgetfulness; of the forgotten past when his love was that of sense, and of memory of the 'one veritable transitory power' which has nevertheless always been *there*. But from this she becomes identified with the ultimate meaning of love. The torments of the temporal, the meaningless, and all the ambivalence of love in its aspect of desire, are transcended in a vision of the Mother of the Word:

> the Garden
> Where all love ends.

From the measured cadences of this hymn we return to the rhythm of the opening passage and the bones sing gladly of their scattering and of their union 'in the quiet of the desert.' The poem ends with further allusions to Ezekiel. God tells the prophet to take two sticks to represent the nations of Joseph and Judah and join them together, 'and they shall be no more two nations, neither shall they be divided into two kingdoms any more at all. . . . This is the land which ye shall divide by lot . . . for inheritance.' But to the bones in their mood of happy assurance the divisions of love into carnal and spiritual no longer seems to matter. It is all one 'area'; now desert, but holding within it the promise of the Garden.

The 'clear visual images' of the third poem give perfect 'sensuous embodiment' to the allegorical content. There is none of the intellectual reasoning of the situation as in the first, though there is the same necessity to 'construct' instead of the spontaneous release of the second poem. In place of the glimpse of grace, and the ecstasy of contemplation, the poet is again enclosed in spiritual darkness. The sense of the slowness of transition from stair to stair and its heavy labour hangs over it all. The 'vapour in the fetid air' is somehow harder to breathe than the air which is 'thoroughly small and dry,' and the turning and twisting, the 'stops and steps of the mind,' and the darkness and silence all create an atmosphere of nightmare. So do the figures seen and suggested. His own vague 'shape,' twisted in struggle with the devil, which brings to mind his picture of Pascal 'facing unflinchingly the demon of doubt which is inseparable from the spirit of belief.' More horrible still the images the narrow darkness turns into. Even the cave in the Waste Land, 'the dead mountain mouth of carious teeth that cannot spit,' is not as physically repulsive as

> an old man's mouth drivelling, beyond repair,
> Or the toothed gullet of an agèd shark.

And the horror within the stairway is intensified by the sensual temptation of the view through the 'slotted window bellied like the fig's fruit,' into the world which in the last poem has been so light-heartedly renounced. Each detail of it emphasizes its opposite in his own plight. Over against the dark imprisonment in the silence and fetid air, the lonely struggle with the devil of the deceitful face, and the pathway into the loathsome mouths, is set the expanse, the colour, the peace, the perfume, the music, the fresh breezes, the 'brown hair over the mouth blown.' But its very enchantment gives added force to the strength of will which continues the climb, and again the poem concludes with the reminder that it is strength beyond that of the individual alone. It is a fragment of the liturgy of the Mass, at the moment before the taking of the Sacrament, which defeats the 'distraction' and focuses the effort on further ascent.

Nowhere is the figure of the Lady so 'complexly opalescent' as in the beautiful fourth poem; not only because of her association with actual colours, but because of the subtle metamorphosis she undergoes in the poet's memory and consciousness, and the dream-like way in which the scenes melt into one another and finally fade away among the 'thousand whispers from the yew.' The echo of the 'between' that haunts the poem adds to this shifting, elusive mobility; 'between the violet and violet,' 'the years that walk between,' 'the time between sleeping and waking,' 'between the yews.' Time and place, dreams and actuality, the desert and the garden, the past and the present, are separate, but interpermeate and interfuse into a sense of vital continuity which can and must be preserved and enriched.

This sense of progression is suggested in the syntax of the opening lines, which continue from some unheard memory of one who, like Beatrice in the *Vita Nuova*, was seen, never to be forgotten. She walks 'between' an actual scene and the world of imaginative vision; between the world of Dante and the poet's own world, among the flowers of a garden and the liturgical colours of the church. She is 'talking of trivial things' in her aspect as a real woman, but holding within her the divine understanding of human suffering, and the source of all vital refreshment and stability, so that the 'eternal dolour' melts into 'colour.'

> Who then made strong the fountains and made
>   fresh the springs
> Made cool the dry rock and made firm the sand
> In blue of larkspur, blue of Mary's colour

From his own 'dolour,' the poet prays to her in the words of Arnaut Daniel. 'Be mindful.'

Again the sense of the flowing continuity of the whole feeling of relationship is evoked in the direct presentation:

> Here are the years that walk between, bearing
> Away the fiddles and the flutes

They pass, bearing away the music-haunted memories of the things of sense, and they are both the years between his own present and his first meeting with the Lady, and the years between his own poem and the poetry of the Middle Ages. They 'restore' his own early experience in the form of a dream figure, wearing 'white light folded, sheathed about her, folded' (like the petals of a rose), and also the memories of all the medieval poets whose allegories are always in the form of dreams. The years walk 'through a bright cloud of tears,' which reminds us of that 'weeping love that implants a new faculty in the heart,' drawing it upwards, of which Dante speaks in the last sonnet of the *Vita Nuova*. They refute the statement of the first poem that

> time is always time
> And place is always and only place,

they assert that all human experience and all poetry are a continuity and a recreation. They are, that is, if time can be 'redeemed,' which may mean bought back, or recovered, or fulfilled.

> Redeem
> The time. Redeem
> The unread vision in the higher dream
> While jewelled unicorns draw by the gilded hearse.

The poet beseeches the Lady to make it possible to recover the spiritual meaning which is 'unread' today in the older poetry. It has become only a 'gilded hearse,' containing the dead body of 'the higher dream.' We see only its external trappings; regard it only as a procession of decorative archaic emblems.

Then the feeling of the procession of the years melts into that of the formal garden, which again is partly that of medieval allegory, partly that of a new symbolic centre of vitality in his own being.[7] The slender yews, general symbols of both mortality and immortality, the garden god, Priapus, fluting of natural and animal fertility, and whose flute is now 'breathless,' blend with the traditional fountain and bird. And between the yews and behind and beyond the pagan god, showing the 'higher dream' of which he is the earthy emblem, the veiled, bright figure 'bent her head and signed but spoke no word.' This is in the tradition of the *amour courtois* of the medieval convention. The first sign of the Lady's grace to her lover was this mere wordless inclination of the head, which nevertheless pledges her to him. Here too the sign of grace renews the fountain of life, and the bird's song takes up the poet's prayer to the Lady to recover and restore the vision which is the 'token' of the reality still 'unheard, unspoken'; the 'word of no speech' in the hymn in the second poem. The

---

[7] The appearance of trees as images, says Jung, are often 'intermediate symbols' in the general archetype of transformation. They represent 'rootedness, repose and growth . . . as also the union of sky and earth.' *Integration of the Personality*, p. 94.

lovely line 'Till the wind shake a thousand whispers from the yew' perhaps refers to the life-giving wind in Ezekiel, or perhaps it means, till we know the secrets of both mortality and immortality.[8]

The liturgical fragment which ends the poem carries on the ambiguity of that. Read as it stands it suggests a return to actuality from the vision contained in the poem; but the full context from the prayer to the Virgin is: 'Turn then, most gracious advocate, thine eyes of mercy towards us. And after this our exile, show unto us the blessed fruit of thy womb, Jesus.'

The next poem is written out of spiritual exile, though it is a different quality of exile from that in *The Hollow Men*. The Lady has been veiled and silent, but her grace has been shown and she has been revealed as the

> Multifoliate rose
> Of death's twilight kingdom

Hence, although here the picture is one of whirling doubt and confusion, and of the impossibility of feeling any living relationship between the noise and darkness and terror and division, and 'the centre of the silent Word,' faith in its *existence* is never in doubt. It is 'within the world and for the world.' The whole sensuous expression, however, is that of the shattering of the calm progression and grouping of all the symbols in the poem before, into a chaotic disorder. There, the past and the present, the lower and the higher love, the desert and the garden, the ancient rhyme and the new verse come together into a rhythmic design where the light, the colours, the silence, the fountain, the bird, the yew trees and the Lady are all absorbed into a central significance; are all composed into a

---

[8] Compare also John iii.8. 'The wind bloweth where it listeth, and thou hearest the sound thereof, but canst not tell whence it cometh, and whither it goeth: so is every one that is born of the Spirit.'

moment which is 'breathless' with the sense of a dawning
revelation.

But here that sense of rhythmical pattern and creative synthesis and assimilation is destroyed; is 'lost.' Both the outer
secular world and the inner world of spirit are alike 'distraction.' But whereas the distraction of the third poem was
accompanied by the achievement of advancing up the spiral
stair, of 'climbing,' however slowly and heavily, here it is mere
'whirling' and chaotic commotion. The light has become the
reiterated, uncomprehending 'darkness'; the silence and the
birdsong, the visionary music of the ancient rhyme, and even
the gay fiddles and the flutes of sensuous music have become
cheapened into a mere mockery of chiming syllables falling on
the outward ear, related to no inner harmony and reverberation.
The 'between' which spelled reconciliation before, now betokens
disruption:

> Those who are torn on the horn between season and
> season, time and time, between
> Hour and hour, word and word, power and power.

And the 'torn' recalls those other aspects of the human plight
which before, in the presence of the Lady, were reconciled
with their opposites. Here the 'distressed,' 'exhausted,' 'worried,' have vanquished the vision of her wholeness; her repose,
her calm, her life-giving silence are lost:

> The right time and the right place are not here
> No place of grace for those who avoid the face
> No time to rejoice for those who walk among noise and
> deny the voice

The 'voice' is the pleading voice of the Lord in his 'contro-
versy with his people.' [9] 'O my people, what have I done unto
thee?' By its incorporation into a penitential ritual for Good
Friday it becomes the voice of Christ speaking out of his
Passion. It is to the Lady that the poet turns for intercession

[9] Micah vi.3.

for himself and for all others in the same conflict, fear and weakness; those who

> cannot surrender
> And affirm before the world and deny between the rocks

And it seems as if his effort to evoke the picture of her between the yew trees does calm him. Just as her whiteness communicated itself to the leopards and the bones, so the rocks here carry the aura of the 'blue of larkspur,' and hence associate themselves with her. The 'last desert' was that in which thoughts of her 'made cool the dry rock and made firm the sand,' and which melted into the garden. Here it may do the same, for 'spitting from the mouth the withered apple-seed' is perhaps the denial of knowledge as the world knows knowledge, and the surrender to 'the voice.'

The whole poem has been in a rhythm of rotation and transition between states of feeling centred in the presence or absence of the Lady. In the first poem her blessèd face and voice are renounced in an act of faith which accepts deprivation itself as creative. In the second the truth of the bare statement of the first is given startling symbolic expression in the rejoicing of the bones and their song. Their joyful feeling of passive accomplishment, however, is contradicted in the third poem, where advance is shown to require more than submission and singing. There 'the deceitful face of hope and of despair,' and the music of the flute, both of which are 'distractions' from the blessèd face and voice, are conquered, but by creative effort not by creative patience. There is a sense here that a station on the way has been passed, and it is immediately followed by the poem in which the Lady's grace is manifested, and accompanied by the glad sensation of release and wholeness; where the 'dreams' blend and end in the brief vision of the Garden. This is the only poem in which the poet actually meets the Lady, and then she remains veiled and silent. It too is followed by

fresh disintegration, by conflict between all the opposing forces
held in 'tension' in the struggle, and the loss of contact with the
only power which can reconcile the whirling antagonisms.

The final poem brings another temporary resolution, but at
the same time a reminder that there is no end to conflict in
the way the poet has chosen. The mere will to submission is
not enough, and to have a vision of the Garden where all love
ends is not to be free of the distracting loves which continue to
haunt 'the dream-crossed twilight between birth and dying.'
The lower dreams remain and can only cease to distract if they
can be absorbed into the higher dream which transcends them.
'The time of tension between dying and birth' is still the time
in which the poem ends. And to point the truth of this, the
'blind eye' of memory sends up another false dream through
the ivory gates of the underworld, and 'the infirm glory of the
positive hour' reasserts itself. The description of it is prefaced
by the 'Bless me father' of the confessional, but it bursts forth
in quickening, rebellious rhythms of rejoicing, in some of the
loveliest lines Eliot has ever written:

> From the wide window towards the granite shore
> The white sails still fly seaward, seaward flying
> Unbroken wings
>
> And the lost heart stiffens and rejoices
> In the lost lilac and the lost sea voices
> And the weak spirit quickens to rebel
> For the bent golden-rod and the lost sea smell
> Quickens to recover
> The cry of quail and the whirling plover . . .
> And smell renews the salt savour of the sandy earth.

Yet it is the 'lost heart' and the 'weak spirit' which are respon-
sible, and who long to restore the old glory of earth and sea,
of colour and movement and sound and smell as enough in
themselves for rejoicing.

But it is 'to mock ourselves with falsehood' to allow that
dream. The poet turns from it to his own dwelling place:

The place of solitude where three dreams cross
Between blue rocks

The Lady is not present and the rocks are not those of 'the granite shore' of happy vision; but they are coloured by her memory, and the living yew trees are a hint of the Garden. The three dreams are perhaps light and dark and twilight, or birth and dying and 'the time of tension.' 'The voices shaken from the yew tree' are the 'sea voices' of the rebellious memory. When they 'drift away,' it is the voice of prayer which is heard again.

The final intercession subtly blends all that has gone before. The full meaning of 'Teach us to care and not to care' comes home to us. There is no struggle between soul and body, only the one struggle towards perfection. The meaning of the yearning towards the sea, just as the meaning of the physical love of woman must be sought in final causes. And again, quite simply 'the final cause is the attraction towards God.' 'Our peace in His will' sends us to the words of Piccarda in the lowest sphere of Paradise, and to the continuation of that speech: 'his will is our peace. It is that sea towards which all moves that it creates and that nature makes.' The poet 'among these rocks' is far from Paradise, and his prayer is still for patience and humility. It is not the glad litany of praise of this second poem, nor the excited appeal for revelation of the fourth; not the impassioned plea of the fifth, nor the acceptance of deprivation of the first. It is the simple prayer that he may express his love in contemplation of the beloved object; a supplication that he may not be *separated* from the knowledge of the 'one veritable transitory power' which has been vouchsafed to him, that beloved and guiding figure who is the *spirit* of life and love, the *spirit* of the fountain, of the garden, of the river, of the sea. And again he identifies himself with all other dwellers among the rocks by making his personal petition to the Lady, and to the 'Thee' of the last line in the traditional words of the prayers of the church.

CHAPTER VIII

Ariel Poems

> For every man who thinks and lives by thought must have his own scepticism, that which stops at the question, that which ends in denial, or that which leads to faith and which is somehow integrated into the faith which transcends it.
>
> T. S. ELIOT. *The 'Pensées' of Pascal.*

DURING the years 1927-9 Eliot not only published two of the parts of *Ash Wednesday* as separate poems, but also *Journey of the Magi, A Song for Simeon* and *Animula.* These, with *Marina,* published in 1931, are known as the Ariel poems. This name, however, is not a title given them by Eliot. It was the name of a series of Christmas poems published over a period of years, to which Eliot contributed, so is without significance in any criticism. All four of the poems embody different aspects of the experience of rebirth, of the discovery of a new focus of existence. They are all visionary impersonal dramatizations of states of feeling within 'the dream-crossed twilight between birth and dying,' this 'time of tension between dying and birth.' And all of them except *Marina* hold this sense of ambiguity between which is which. The passage between the death of the old and the birth of the new is marked by no milestone. It is 'this birth season of decease,' a condition of suspension between the two: it is a 'transit,' a 'journey.' Emotionally, it is equivocal and indefinite, 'wavering between the profit and the loss.' The meaning of the new birth is obscure, full of doubt, accompanied by pain, not joy, and perplexing in the extreme.[1]

This is particularly true of the first poem, *Journey of the Magi*. The opening is a direct quotation from one of the Nativity sermons of Lancelot Andrewes, and the method of the poem follows a pattern which Eliot discerns in Andrewes' prose. 'Before extracting all the spiritual meaning of a text, Andrewes forces a concrete presence upon us.' The experience is projected first in direct realistic terms; terms of bad weather and the practical details of hardships and antagonisms. There is no mention of the dream or the star of the Gospel story. In memory, one of the Magi recounts the incident, in all the extraordinary precision and clarity of its external detail, and in all the uncertainty and obscurity of its ultimate significance. The tone is direct, conversational, factual: the dominating feeling that of faith without revelation. The determined faith, never openly stated, comes through the description of the character of the journey and its results. In the background are the 'Kingdoms' the wise men left:

> There were times we regretted
> The summer palaces on slopes, the terraces,
> And the silken girls bringing sherbet.

But this 'regret' is the only personal emotion expressed in the opening section of the poem. Everything else is communicated by the simple enumeration, without comment, of the things that had to be endured. One after another, (there are twelve uses of 'and' in the first fifteen lines), follow all the obstacles provided by both nature and man to oppose and frustrate the journey, 'and such a long journey.' Each is a vivid picture of delay or embarrassment or obstruction. First there are the

[1] 'The birth of the deliverer is equivalent to a great catastrophe since a new and powerful life issues forth just when no life or force or new development was anticipated . . . This reversal of values is tantamount to a destruction of previously accepted values; hence it resembles a devastation. . . .' Jung. *Psychological Types,* p. 328.

hindrances of nature; the cold, the bad roads, the sore-footed camels 'lying down in the melting snow.' But in addition to these are all the exasperations arising from the active and passive frailties of man:

> Then the camel men cursing and grumbling
> And running away, and wanting their liquor and women,
> And the night-fires going out, and the lack of shelters,
> And the cities hostile and the towns unfriendly
> And the villages dirty and charging high prices:

The narrator expresses no rebellion at all this. All he remembers is the faith that impelled them forward, the sense of urgency which made them quicken their pace, and which conquered not only the practical impediments and their own fatigue, but also their own doubts:

> the voices singing in our ears, saying
> That this was all folly.

In the second stanza the images become symbolic as well as realistic, though the extension is subtle and unobtrusive. The narrator continues to report faithfully the external details of the scene, as if they had face value only, but some of these hold a significance for the reader beyond that perceived by the travellers. The new way is different both from the old summer ease and luxury and from the struggle through the darkness, 'sleeping in snatches,' of the cold winter journey. The rhythm softens and flows more easily. There is dawn and dampness and the smell of growing things, and a sudden intensification of assurance: 'with a running stream and a water-mill beating the darkness.' The water and the mill are both vital forces, full of throbbing, driving life, with all the practical and symbolic activity carried by '*beating* the darkness'; denying the voices saying that this was all folly. They and the fertile valley and the trees and the 'old white horse galloping away in a

meadow,' and the vine-leaves over the door of the tavern, all
speak of hope and freedom and fruitfulness; but again they are
qualified by the implied vision of the three 'trees' on Golgotha,
and the reminder of greed and treachery in the glimpse of the
'six hands at an open door dicing for pieces of silver.' [2] The
transposing of memories of the crucifixion, of the dicing for
Christ's garments and the thirty pieces of silver, to the approach to the scene of the birth foreshadows the basic ambiguity of the conclusion. The hope of the 'dawn' in this new
land is not crowned by any scene of adoration or of rejoicing
'with great joy.' On the contrary the narrator's comment,
though it may be read to imply fulfilment if we take 'satisfactory' in its literal sense, carries none of that sense. It is a bald
recitation of the ending of a quest, not in failure, but in anti-
climax and inadequacy:

> But there was no information, and so we continued
> And arrived at evening, not a moment too soon
> Finding the place; it was (you may say) satisfactory.

There was no illumination; only a bewildering sense of paradox, expressed with fierce intensity:

> I would do it again, but set down
> This set down
> This: were we led all that way for
> Birth or Death?

The birth brought 'hard and bitter agony,' far beyond the hardships of the journey. It brought the death of 'the old dispensation,' with its unthinking ease; the sense of alienation from
their own people, who had 'roots that clutch' in their old ways;

---

[2] 'Why, for all of us, out of all that we have heard, seen, felt, in a
lifetime, do certain images recur, charged with emotion, rather than
others? . . . six ruffians seen through an open window playing cards at
night at a small French railway junction where there was a water-mill.'
The Use of Poetry and the Use of Criticism, p. 148.

so that it is in their own country now that they find 'the cities hostile and the towns unfriendly.' The faith remains: 'we had evidence and no doubt,' but their journey seems to have had no *creative* significance and to have brought no creative change. There is no water-mill beating the darkness in their land. There is only great weariness and disillusionment in the last line, 'I should be glad of another death.'

In *A Song for Simeon* there is the same emotional pattern. The birth of the new Word destroys the pattern of 'the old dispensation,' but though Simeon *sees* where salvation lies, he is too old and tired to create anything himself. He wants only peace, and knows that it is only death that will bring it. Any life left to him means only the knowledge that it is not peace but a sword which is to be the lot of the true followers of 'the still unspeaking and unspoken word.' Others will reach the 'consolation' which is the reward of the inevitable suffering of creative living and dying, but that is not for him.

The voice which speaks in the poem is very different from that of the narrator of *Journey of the Magi*. The vigorous, graphic descriptions, the moments of excited intensity, and the lapses into weary bafflement, all alike carried in the tones of direct speech, are gone. In their place is a more musical rhythm, direct biblical echoes, chant-like cadences and irregular rhyme and assonance. Simeon's state of suspension between dying and birth, between birth and dying, is beautifully created in the rhythm of the first stanza. Again the distinction between the two states is blurred: 'the stubborn season has made stand' may mean either the winter or the spring. What is sure is that Simeon himself cannot partake of the 'stubbornness' of either. He is passive, detached, waiting:

> My life is light, waiting for the death wind,
> Like a feather on the back of my hand.
> Dust in sunlight and memory in corners
> Wait for the wind that chills towards the dead land.

And the time of waiting is now haunted by the pain and disquiet of the revelation. There is none of the suggestion in the Gospel story that the vision 'revealed unto him by the Holy Ghost that he should not see death before he had seen the Lord's Christ,' brings any sense of triumph. It merely brings the knowledge that all his 'just and devout' past life, on which he had complacently prided himself, is a pattern in which he is 'no longer at ease.' In place of contented old age there is the consciousness of the coming 'time of sorrow' and of its continuance, and of the fact that the creative sacrifice of the saints cannot be his, though he can contemplate it. In this Simeon does differ from the Magi. To both, the new birth remains pure loss as far as their own lives are concerned. Both recognize it, but not with the joyful prophecy of 'Unto us a child is born, unto us a son is given.' With the Magi it is accompanied by no social change whatever: with Simeon it brings the vision of the pain, death and destruction which is to be the *immediate* conclusion of the birth of the new value. He does however also see its dynamic power as a potential new intensity of living. The rhythm quickens as he begins to describe the glimpse of the *mounting,* the glory and the ecstasy; but it is checked and slowed again at once by the intrusion of his own impotence.

> They shall praise Thee and suffer in every generation
> With glory and derision,
> Light upon light, mounting the saints' stair.
> Not for me the martyrdom, the ecstasy of thought and
>   prayer,
> Not for me the ultimate vision.

He repeats his plea for peace, for release from the new disturbing consciousness, knowing that death alone can bring it. What remains of his old life is now meaningless because it can have 'no tomorrow.' It is not peace, it is merely the heavy burden of realization that both in himself and in the majority of mankind, what he had called life, is death; and moreover that even for those who have a 'tomorrow' life and death seem indistinguishable from one another.

> I am tired with my own life and the lives of those after
>   me,
> I am dying in my own death and the deaths of those
>   after me.

Animula [3] carries on the same theme of the difficulty of distinguishing the true pattern, indeed of its impossibility without a spiritual death prefaced by the viaticum, the sacramental symbol of the passage from death to the rebirth of the soul, and of the provision for that journey. Here it is no longer a dramatic impersonator who speaks the lines. The uneven rhythms of the two old men change to sustained poetic statement in flowing, supple lines, cunningly rhymed and varied by innumerable changes of stress and of the number of syllables to a line.

The quotation at the opening is from the sixteenth canto of the *Purgatorio* where Marco Lombardo discourses to Dante on the need for spiritual law vested in the Church to guide the innocent childish soul into true development. From this suggestion of the soul as child, Eliot passes to a description of the world of childhood, creating living sense impressions of its unthinking joys and fears, its instability of movement and emotion, its incapacity to distinguish between 'actual and fanciful.' The child lives by instinct only, but its life flows free and uninhibited; it is full of movement in its own being or delight in the movement around it, 'the wind, the sunlight or the sea' or 'running stags around a silver tray.' From this simple, dynamic world, ruled only by the instincts, time forces upon the growing soul a world full of the unpleasant necessities of distinguishing between reality and illusion, of trying

[3] The title recalls Hadrian's lines to his poor little wandering soul, 'animula, vagula, blandula . . .'

to understand the accepted prohibitions and freedoms, and of moral choice. The 'heavy burden' of these problems 'perplexes and offends more, day by day.' The soul gives up the struggle to grow; it is simpler to remain childish, to compensate 'the pain of living' with 'the drug of dreams,' to shelter behind the world's definition of knowledge:

> The pain of living and the drug of dreams
> Curl up the small soul in the window seat
> Behind the *Encyclopaedia Britannica.*

The inevitable result of this is the adult body with the spiritual and moral equipment of a child. In childhood, the limitations of movement and the sense of emotional insecurity are natural, and are recompensed by ever-present reassurance of love from outside itself; the soul can live fully in the unsullied delights of the senses and the innocent contemplation of the patterns of nature or art or dreams. But 'the hand of time' is very different from 'the hand of God.' Instead of time moulding the soul in loving understanding of

> the imperatives of 'is and seems'
> And may and may not, desire and control

it teaches it nothing. The soul issues from it with all its spontaneous joys warped, all its potentialities frustrated; its fears comforted by no love, its being denied any 'warm reality,' its delight in light and life annihilated to complete nonentity, without substance or pattern,

> Shadow of its own shadows, spectre in its own gloom,
> Leaving disordered papers in a dusty room;

The conclusion would be that of *The Hollow Men* were it not for the completion of the sentence.

> Living first in the silence after the viaticum.

There are many whose first death is 'Death, our death,' and whose life throughout is a mere process of dying. But since even such souls issued originally from the hand of God, they must return with the possibility of purgation. The possibility breaks the calm statement of the hopelessness of the souls who are mere shadows and spectres, and the poet adds an urgent prayer for those who have passed into physical death without the viaticum, perishing in the 'misshapen' temporal patterns they created for themselves. All are clear except 'Floret, by the boarhound slain between the yew trees.' The picture seems to be of one who, unlike the others, was aware of the ambiguity of life and death: he stood 'between the yew trees.' Perhaps he was slain by the animal in him. These yew trees stand neither among the rocks or in a garden. The last line ironically emphasizes again that the hour of birth and of dying may be the same.

'Andrewes takes a word and derives the world from it; squeezing and squeezing the word until it yields a full juice of meaning which we should never have supposed any word to possess.' Eliot has been doing the same thing with the words *birth* and *death* in these poems, forcing the consciousness of the reader to feel with him their equivocal connotations. But it is the full meaning of *death* which heavily preponderates. The sense of new life is faint and fitful, and the faith in it, though fixed and steady, supports itself with no *emotional* assurance. Eliot says again of Andrewes' style that 'it may seem pedantic and verbal. It is only when we have saturated ourselves in his prose . . . that we find his examination of words terminating in the ecstasy of assent.' It would be possible to say that in the early Ariel poems the faith in the reality of rebirth may seem 'pedantic and verbal'; but it is certainly true that it terminates in *Marina* in 'the ecstasy of assent.'

It is interesting too that it is no vision of the Christian

Nativity which brings the overwhelming sense of emotional certainty to Eliot, but that of a very different child. According to Jung the revelation of the beginning of new spiritual experience is usually heralded by the appearance in dreams of some sort of miraculous child, symbolizing the new potentiality for growth and development which has awakened in the unconscious. 'Psychologically, the divine birth heralds the fact that a new symbol, a new expression of supreme vital intensity is being created . . . from this moment the supreme intensity of life is to be found only upon the new line. Every other direction falls gradually away, dissolving into oblivion.[4] It is this feeling of supreme vital intensity which radiates from the poem. It is the only purely joyous poem Eliot has ever written. The joy is not that of a triumphant moment of passionate fulfilment, but the profound and exquisite joy of a moment when, out of confusion, heaviness and despair, the world is suddenly transformed into beauty and significance. The possibilities are too complex and elusive to become explicit to the poet; the pattern cannot be fully comprehended. Its various elements, the images that return, seem unrelated, dream-like, and the speaker can only enumerate their harmonious presences and communicate the sense of free-flowing streamlike association which enfolds them all and unites them in the figure of Marina.

In an unpublished address on 'Shakespeare as Poet and Dramatist'[5] Eliot wrote: 'To my mind the finest of all the "recognition scenes" is Act V: i of that very great play *Pericles.* It is a perfect example of the "ultra-dramatic," a dramatic action of beings who are more than human . . . It is the speech of creatures who are more than human, or rather, seen in a light more than that of day.' Eliot's poem has the same lighting, and his Marina is more than human. She is the dream-symbol of something newly born, and the scene is a recogni-

---

[4] *Psychological Types,* p. 235.
[5] Given at Edinburgh University in 1937.

tion, a discovery of this magical creative regeneration, begotten in some mysterious way by the speaker himself. With a strange ironic twist, Eliot has chosen an epigraph from the *Hercules Furens* of Seneca, telling of the moment when Hercules, having unknowingly killed his children in a fit of madness, returns to sanity, questions where he is, and is forced to recognize the deaths he has himself caused. It is no more ironic however than *Journey of the Magi*. There, though birth is the theme we associate with the subject matter, it is death which pervades the consciousness of the speaker. Here too, as always in Eliot, death and birth are very close. Not only the epigraph, but the setting of the Pericles story reminds us of it. Marina was born at sea, then believed to have been murdered by those in whose charge she was left, and miraculously restored to her father when she was a grown woman. Pericles therefore has already experienced the belief that she was dead, and it is not only the sudden, unexpected presence of life when death had been accepted, but the return of life transfigured and transformed, matured out of all knowing, which is the miracle.

The poem illustrates very strikingly how in the poetic imagination, as in dreams, images already deeply felt, and active as symbols of great psychic importance, can rearrange themselves into a new constellation as it were, having a completely new intensity of value and significance. Here the sea and the memory of the sights and sounds and scents of the seacoast, and the figure of a woman, all of which came together in the last poem of *Ash Wednesday,* regroup themselves in an atmosphere entirely different. There, the controlling element was that of a religious discipline, gladly accepted, but nevertheless subduing the rebellious senses to the contemplation of a divine source, and framed in a ritual observance aimed to concentrate consciousness on that source. Here the one word 'grace' though not confined to a religious context, carries a hint of it. But it is the release from the *confinement* of the religious context which creates the new world of the poem and liberates the new life in it. It is a spontaneous uprush of the sense of a new reality, intangible, and in a way inexpressible, but apprehended as

> This form, this face, this life
> Living to live in a world of time beyond me.

And there is a vast difference in the quality of the *anima* figure as she appears as the Lady in *Ash Wednesday* and in *Marina*. In both she is 'opalescent,' a semi-visionary companion, yet holding within her being the *meaning* of the total experience. But again, here she has lost the *formal* element of a poetic and religious tradition. She is not semi-divine 'sister,' 'mother,' veiled, remote, worshipful; she is 'daughter,' both child and woman, created of the speaker, springing from himself, a part of himself, though strange, unfamiliar, and re-created of his spirit.

She is of the sea, and the recognition of her presence associates itself with a scene of peace and loveliness, where rocks have none of the connotation they carry in *Ash Wednesday:*

> What seas what shores what grey rocks and what
>   islands
> What water lapping the bow
> And scent of pine and the woodthrush singing through
>   the fog
> What images return
> O my daughter.

Then in a strange, chant-like progression, all ideas associated with the sensual or lustful aspects of love, dissolve: the 'insubstantial pageant' fades. They are 'reduced,' which carries with it so many meanings: they are diminished, subdued, re-ordered and appear in a new combination of values. They have been

> reduced by a wind,
> A breath of pine, and the woodsong fog

And 'by this grace dissolved in place,' which holds the double
meaning that their substance has been dissolved by this
miraculous presence, and that the miraculous presence pervades everything. The place and the presence melt into one
another and are inseparable. But the poet (or the fictitious
Pericles) tries to define the character of the miracle.

> What is this face, less clear and clearer
> The pulse in the arm, less strong and stronger—
> Given or lent? more distant than stars and nearer than
>   the eye

It is new life, unlike the old life of the physical senses and
yet at the same time a heightening and enhancement of it:
something intensely personal yet diffused throughout the
universe.[6] Whether a permanent possession or a mere fugitive
visitant, it brings with it a joyous spontaneity and excitement
and a sense of movement and delight which is associated with
some childhood memory. The 'whispers and small laughter
between leaves and hurrying feet' is part of a memory which
is created in the short lyric *New Hampshire,* and recurs in
Four Quartets, and is charged with a half-comprehended sense
of ecstasy. It returns in that dream world where all the streams
of images from the conscious and the unconscious, the past
and the present, meet and flow and reform into new patterns.

Then with all the unaccountable pattern of dream, we hear
of the strange ship whose bow the water is lapping. The sea-
world and the dream-world meet. Pericles and Marina are
together on this very insecure and dilapidated vessel, which
seems quite out of keeping with the perfection of the ex-

---

[6] Compare Jung on the sense of possessing a new psychic reality: 'It
is strange to us and yet so near, quite our own and yet unknowable.'

perience. But the significance of it is in the 'I made this.'[7]
The presence of Marina is in some strange way connected with
a constructive effort of his own. The ship has come through
bad times, it is defective and damaged, and its building was
carried through over a long period of unawareness of its purpose; it was no planned, rational creation of the will. But
though he made it 'unknowing, half-conscious, unknown,' it is
'my own.' It has been the *means* which has brought Marina to
him, and having served its purpose, it too can now dissolve,
for his whole being is centred on the vision she evokes:

>   let me
> Resign my life for this life, my speech for that
>   unspoken,
> The awakened, lips parted, the hope, the new ships.

The sea voices and the sea smell, the birdsong calling and the
granite shores are no longer reminders of the lost heart and the
weak rebellious spirit. The worlds of sense and spirit are one;
'the time of tension' is transformed into a moment of complete
release; the solitude among the rocks into the rapture of the
presence of Marina. She, like the Lady, does not speak, but
she is 'the warm reality, the offered good,' and the poem ends
in 'the ecstasy of assent' to the new life and love, to a glad
surrender to wherever the voyage may lead:

> What seas what shores what granite islands towards my
>   timbers
> And woodthrush calling through the fog
> My daughter.

[7] As a human construction, the ship has the meaning (in the dream
sequence of 'transformation') of a system, method or way. Jung, *Integration of the Personality*, p. 189.

CHAPTER IX

Coriolan

It is my contention that we have today a culture
which is mainly negative, but which, so far as it is
positive, is still Christian. I do not think that it can
remain negative, because a negative culture has ceased
to be efficient in a world where economic as well as
spiritual forces are proving the efficiency of cultures
which, even when pagan, are positive; and I believe that
the choice before us is between the formation of a new
Christian culture, and the acceptance of a pagan one.

T. S. ELIOT.   *The Idea of a Christian Society*

MARINA creates the revelation of a new centre of consciousness, a new supreme significance. This brings
an extraordinary intensity of feeling, which is at once
that of recognition and of renewal. The old world is not lost,
but it is transfigured. The same experience, in part, was created
in the fourth poem of *Ash Wednesday*, but there the whole experience is centred in the figure of the Lady. It is, as Eliot
said of the figure of Beatrice in the *Vita Nuova*, 'something
related to what we now call sublimation.' It wove into living
poetry the sense of the absorption of a part of the self formerly
projected upon living woman, into a total response to a
religious belief. The whole consciousness of the poet is focussed
on the shining clarity and loveliness of the Lady, which again
becomes centralized in religious feeling by the liturgical fragment of the conclusion.

But in *Marina* the movement is quite different. The intensity of feeling is no less, but it is diffused over a much
wider area. The force is centrifugal instead of centripetal. It

132

moves outwards from the central figure, and though controlled from that centre, radiates from it in all directions. The 'grace' is no longer in the Lady's gesture, it is 'dissolved in place'; Marina does not wear 'white light folded, sheathed about her, folded,' so that all the light is absorbed into her. Instead, while remaining herself, she becomes a part of a new lighting of the old world; something 'more distant than the stars and nearer than the eye.' And she is as much a part of the poet himself as she is of the seas, the shores, the rocks, the islands and 'the scent of pine and the woodthrush singing through the fog.' The unity she symbolizes enfolds the individual and the universe.

> This form, this face, this life
> Living to live in a world of time beyond me. Let me
> Resign my life for this life.

But it is in a poem published in the following year, a poem of a completely different character, that Eliot first creates the symbol of this new vision as a new *dimension* in living, a 'still point in a turning world.' *Triumphal March* is the first in a series of poems which were to have had the general title *Coriolan,* but only two of the series were published. In them he set out to dramatize a vision of the world of actuality in the light of his new apprehension of a 'reality' which transcended it, but in which, could it but recognize it, the world has its truest life. In *Marina* the whole emphasis is on this reality as a new living *presence* in personal living; in the Coriolan poems the emphasis is on its *absence* in any view of the world as a pattern of temporal, objective relationships. Very subtly, and entirely in poetic image and association, Eliot contrasts a world structure focussed finally on the visible Hero as the centre of a vast organization of force, with that hidden point which is the central light of another world.

The poem throughout is a masterpiece of inter-related contrasts. The stillness of the still point holds in itself properties of time and space in direct opposition to those of the turning world at any point in history. For the purposes of the poem the time and space of 'history' is collapsed to a 'day' which is equally Roman and contemporary.[1] The succeeding events of this day, and the procession itself, that is, the external world as a *sequence* of moments, is juxtaposed to the eternal 'noon' hidden at the heart of a different concept of time and movement. In the same way the 'perceiving' which is 'the natural wakeful life of our Ego' is contrasted with the intuitive apprehension of the different pattern of reality.

The 'day' of the poem is no ordinary day. 'We hardly knew ourselves that day or knew the City.' It is a day into which the whole essence of a civilization is distilled. And the qualities of that civilization are communicated to us by an intricate interweaving of facts and suggestions in the apparently simple but cunningly ironic monologue of one of the crowd watching the parade. Indeed 'he's artful' would be a good description of Eliot's method. He has been so careful to try and prevent the interpretation of the poem as political satire at the expense of totalitarianism. The unexpected entrance of the line, 'The natural wakeful life of our Ego is a perceiving,' in the middle of the account of the waiting crowd at once directs the lens. 'Our Ego' is nothing very distant.

The magnificent opening, repeated later, concentrates the quintessence of it all.

Stone, bronze, stone, steel, stone, oakleaves, horses' heels
    Over the paving.

With this ringing echo of unyielding hardness in our ears, and with the sight and sound of the other symbols of military glory, the numberless flags and trumpets and eagles, we become aware of the crowd itself, 'such a press of people,' all 'waiting'

[1] Eliot has spoken of the contemporary scene as 'more analogous to that of the later Roman Empire than to any other period that we know.'

on 'the way to the temple,' until 'he' comes. 'So many waiting, how many waiting? What did it matter on such a day?' It does not matter, for the individual as an organic unit in the whole no longer matters. 'What comes first?' is the next question, and the answer is the enumeration of the weapons of war and the ammunition and the whole equipment of the army. This is followed by the organized bands of the sporting elements and then by the municipal officers. We see the picture of a whole society where the mechanical destructive force man has created 'comes first,' with man himself organized into pieces of social machinery, and the unthinking 'people,' provided they have their 'stools and sausages,' question nothing beyond what they 'see.'

Then the great moment:

Look

> There he is now, look:
> There is no interrogation in his eyes
> Or in the hands, quiet over the horse's neck,
> And the eyes watchful, waiting, perceiving, indifferent.

The Hero differs only in one respect from the crowd. He too is 'watchful, waiting, perceiving,' but he is 'indifferent,' and 'there is no interrogation in his eyes' or in his hands. He cares nothing for the people who hail him as saviour, and his vision sees nothing and questions nothing beyond the pattern of values of which he is the central symbol, and which his 'hands' translate into government or command. The other central symbol is hidden:

> O hidden under the dove's wing, hidden in the turtle's
>   breast,
> Under the palmtree at noon, under the running water
> At the still point of the turning world. O hidden.

The procession goes on to the temple. 'Then the sacrifice,' and the deadness of everything in the religious observance is symbolised in the urns and the four times reiterated 'Dust,' and related immediately to the repetition of the opening lines of the poem.

'That is all we could see,' says the speaker. It is left to the reader to compare the suggestions created in the lines on what is 'hidden' with what has been 'seen.' In the place of the inflexible hardness of the stone, bronze, steel, we feel the softness of the dove and turtle feathers, the pliant grace of the palmtree; instead of the rigidly regimented procession, the running water; instead of the deadness and dust, organic life. But beyond these contrasts in sense-perception, there are all the elusive implications scattered in the conclusion of the poem, enforcing its inner significance. Already the hint of the palmtree has brought to mind the ironic parallel of a very different triumphant procession with the multitudes waiting on the way to the temple to see 'him' pass, riding on an ass. The ironic pressure increases with the fragment of talk which places the temple and the sacrifice in its modern context, and illustrates the 'dust' into which the Christian tradition has disintegrated. Its symbolic language is so 'undecipherable' that to the literal-minded Cyril the ringing of the bell at the elevation of the Host can be translated only into memories of the muffin and crumpet man ringing his bell in the London streets. The ignoring of the food of the spirit in favour of that of the body is hinted again in the 'Don't throw away that sausage,/It'll come in handy.' The arrangement of the words in the next phrase,

> Please, will you
> Give us a light?
> Light
> Light

turns the commonplace request into a prayer that what is 'hidden' may be revealed. But the last quotation, with its picture of the lines of soldiers drawn up in formation with their bayonets facing each other, emphasizes the 'hedge' that blocks the vision, ever growing greater just as the letters enlarge themselves at the conclusion.

We can guess that one reason for abandoning the *Coriolan* sequence was the difficulty of the dramatic monologue form for the purpose Eliot had in hand. Their only weakness is that the speakers in the poems would not dramatically have Eliot's own apprehension of the still point in the turning world, being entirely preoccupied with its turning. Their 'perceiving' is all on the level of the natural wakeful life of our Ego, and though a great part of the 'meaning' can be introduced by the satiric irony with which the speakers, all unaware, reveal much more than they say, still the crucial lines creating the new vision in *Triumphal March* are dramatically inappropriate in the mouth of the supposed speaker. *The Difficulties of a Statesman* is more successful in that way, since the poor harassed politician is nearer Eliot's own degree of sensibility. But by making it more straightforwardly dramatic the real purpose of creating an apprehension of, and directing attention to, the 'still point,' is largely lost in the flow of the tragi-comedy of dramatic self-revelation.

The satire in this, with the refrain 'What shall I cry?' blending the official power and private despair of the speaker, is excellent sardonic fun. The robust ridicule of bureaucratic administration, and of the clash between public and private ambitions reaches its culmination in the complete impasse:

> A commission is appointed
> To confer with a Volscian commission
> About perpetual peace: the fletchers and javelin-makers
>   and smiths
> Have appointed a joint committee to protest against
>   the reduction of orders.

The rest of the poem expands the contrasts already 'given' in *Triumphal March*. The new refrain 'O mother' suggests the baffled desire for some directing and loving authority to appeal to, and at the same time the essential immaturity of the direction it takes. Whereas *Triumphal March* indicated a *wrong* centre on which public attention is focussed, *Difficulties of a Statesman* creates the opposite error of a complete *lack of centre*. The wrong centre appears again in 'the row of family portraits, dingy busts, all looking remarkably Roman,' but the only alternative to *that* pattern is the dissolving confusion of committee on committee and the vain hope that correct observance of sacrifice and submission to the gods—'the mactations, immolations, oblations, impetrations'—may have some magic force.

> Meanwhile the guards shake dice on the marches
> And the frogs (O Mantuan) croak in the marshes.

The '(O Mantuan)' reminds us that while Virgil chronicled the glories of Rome, it too had within it the seeds of its own decay; its enervating inattention to its corporate life, its malarial swamps. Then too, the frogs croaked their reminders of doom.

All through the rest of the poem Eliot plants in the reader's mind the *smallness* (to the statesman and his world) of the reminders of a different order of consciousness, but hints to us at the same time that this order, however miniature its manifestations and fitful its appearance, has the continuity and permanence which marks natural vitality as opposed to the melancholy muddle of human affairs. The central light is shaded, 'set under the upper branches of noon's widest tree,' and fitful as 'the small flare of the firefly or lightning bug,' but it is essentially different in *character* from that on the dingy busts 'lit up successfully by the flare/Of a sweaty torch-bearer, yawning.' The stir of 'the small wind after noon,' 'the sweep of the little bat's wing,' the thin chirp of the small creatures through the dust, is more significant than the 'cry.' The source of the life 'where the dove's foot rested and locked for a moment,' where 'the cyclamen spreads its wings [and] the clematis droops over the lintel,' is 'hidden,' but it is very different in kind from the confused, restless perplexities driving the worried statesman. In the final 'cry' of the repeated 'RESIGN,' with its condensation of political implication with the echo from *Marina* we hear Eliot's ironic comment on the futilities of statesmanship without a centre in some reality more permanent and more satisfying to the nature of man than that of government machinery.

CHAPTER X

◆◈◆

Four Quartets

If we learn to read poetry properly, the poet never
persuades us to believe anything . . . What we learn
from Dante, or the Bhagavad-gita, or any other religious
poetry is what it *feels* like to believe that religion.

T. S. ELIOT. *Address at Concord Academy 1947*

IN a quotation from Jung in the first chapter of this book [1]
he attempts to give some idea of the new centre of being
attained by the process of 'transformation' which results
in the integration of the personality. He describes the intuitive
nature of perception through which this centre is apprehended,
and its character as an experience of pattern and control. He
adds: 'Visualizations are never more than awkward attempts
of a fumbling mind to give some form to the inexpressible
psychological facts.' The visualizations which he is here
referring to are dream images which characterize the final
phase of the whole 'archetype of transformation.' This archetype, since in his description of it, it is being lived, not
fashioned into art, is in no sense a procession of clear 'primordial images,' the myth of a Quest or a Pilgrim's Progress.
Throughout, there is synthesis as well as sequence. The single
images within the whole experience 'are not isolated from each
other in the unconscious but are in a state of the most complete
mutual interpenetration and interfusion.' But in spite of this,
if the conscious will is collaborating with the revelations contained in the dream symbols, Jung traces an apparently purposive sequence of images creating the gradual shift from the

[1] See page 13.

ego as the centre of being, to a different centre. It begins with
the going down into the darkness, to the water, the mythical
theme of the hero's journey under the sea or a lake, or in the
belly of a beast, or as a Fisher King. It means a meeting with
the Shadow, actually the inner realities of a man's own unconscious, however it may be transposed into monsters and
dragons and ordeals. It means a repudiation of the old practical
guides of the ego, and the allowing of the ego to be object
not subject; the experience of 'not doing.' The new centre
of value will then reveal itself under the image of some form
of enclosure, which to Jung has the meaning of the Greek
temenos, an isolated sacred place; visualized in dream as garden, courtyard or such. At the same time, the anima figure
makes its appearance, symbol of the woman element in man,
with which he must come to terms if he is to develop further.
Images of a miraculous child and the sensations of renewal
through it come from the unconscious. The anima figure becomes increasingly depersonalized, as the feminine function
she represents becomes integrated into the total response of the
personality, and diffuses itself throughout consciousness. More
and more, dramatic figures as actors cease to appear as symbols
of the new centre, and it reveals itself as abstract pattern, in
dream symbols of plastic design which bring extraordinary
sensations of release, assurance and 'rightness.'

What they bring is, according to Jung, the sense of *wholeness*
of personality, the Self in place of the Ego. The deepest
feelings of the Ego become its assurance of relationship with
the Self, a relationship which can only be 'sensed' since wholeness of personality is an ideal which is humanly unattainable;
which can be experienced only through its parts. Moreover it
is a feeling which develops very gradually and becomes a part
of experience at the cost of great effort, and is at once 'task
and goal.' Efforts to visualize the fleeting images in drawings
take most varied forms, but according to Jung, have always
certain elements in the design which are constant. They are in

the form of what he calls a *mandala*. He says that mandala is a Sanskrit word meaning magic circle, and that the basic design includes always a circle, having a centre, and divided into four equal parts.

> This design has turned up in every cultural region, more or less, and we find it today not only in Christian churches, but in Tibetan monasteries as well. It is the so-called sun-wheel, and as it dates from a time when no one had thought of wheels as a mechanical device, it cannot have its source in any experience of the external world. It is rather a symbol that stands for a psychic happening; it covers an experience of the inner world.[2]

Jung asserts that the mandala dream image always combines the elements of a circular rotation, (frequently of rotating light), some element of 'fourness,' and the all-important centre. Whereas in its consciously religious art-forms in West and East, the centre will have the figure of Christ or Buddha, (generally within the design of rose or lotus), the secular unconscious seems generally to produce some natural symbolic emblem such as flower, sun, star, or pool of water.[3] But he regards all such manifestations as 'expressions of a certain attitude which we cannot avoid calling religious.' . . . 'Religion is a relationship to the highest and strongest value . . . The relationship is voluntary as well as involuntary, that is, you can accept consciously the value by which you are possessed unconsciously.'[4]

In the mandala pattern, the circle suggests the imagined wholeness of being, and the centre the point at which the resolution of opposites occurs which makes such a sense of wholeness possible. For Jung sees the pattern of 'reality' in

---

[2] 'Psychology and Literature.' *Modern Man in Search of a Soul*, p. 188.

[3] Iconographers tell me that the mandala is a Chinese pattern only, and that reproductions of Indian and Christian pictorial designs which Jung in his books calls mandalas are not recognized as such by them.

[4] *Psychology and Religion*, p. 98.

the Heraclitean terms of a dynamic system in which a central energy perpetuates itself by opposing forces which, though apparently antitheses, are found to be phases of one cyclical process. As Heraclitus says: 'The unlike is joined together and from differences result most beautiful harmony, and all things take place by strife.' Heraclitus too, though he had no concept of a round world in which to place his imagery of pattern, saw the four elements as alternatively predominating constituents of one universe. Jung traces the insistence upon 'fourness' which the mandala dreams and drawings always possess, to some inexplicable constituent in the unconscious mind which is constantly asserting itself in symbol. He calls it 'the archetypal image of God as manifested in his creation,' citing the visions of Ezekiel and the Apocalypse as literary illustrations. He comments: 'The central Christian symbolism is a Trinity, but the formula of the unconscious mind is a quaternity.[5] To the unconscious there seems to be something wholer about fourness than threeness.

Jung's speculations about the mandala imagery have led, as he says, to the accusation that he is 'mystical.' His reply is that if so, it is because the 'mystical' idea is enforced by the natural and spontaneous occurrences of the unconscious mind, which, he has found, always produce the same kind of symbolism to give vision and sensation to a certain attitude of consciousness which produces harmonious living. He is careful to make it clear that he is not attempting to prove the existence of God through the presence of mandalas. 'They prove only the existence of an archetypal image of the Deity, which to my mind is the most we can assert psychologically about God. But as it is a very important and influential archetype, its relatively frequent occurrence seems to be a noteworthy fact for any theologia naturalis.' [6]

[5] *Two Essays on Analytical Psychology*, p. 265.
[6] *Psychology and Religion*, p. 73.

It will be clear to those familiar with *Four Quartets* that Eliot's imagined circle and 'still point' have what Jung calls the mandala form, though any materials supplied by the unconscious would only confirm what Eliot had already accepted intellectually: psychology is the handmaid and not the housekeeper of theology. Eliot too is frequently accused of 'mysticism,' a word loosely used nowadays, and associated almost always with emotional experiences unrelated to any intellectual and moral discipline. Eliot's 'mysticism' is never of this nature, as he has tried to make clear in his prose writings. He is in the tradition of those Christian and Oriental mystics who have believed that moments of intuitive insight into the nature of 'reality' come as the crown to 'prayer, observance, discipline, thought and action.' His poetry from *Gerontion* onwards is a record of the gradual development from the position where his *intellect* accepted Christian dogma, through the stages by which intellectual acceptance grew painfully and arduously into a conviction embracing the totality of personal and social experience. As he says himself: 'a religious "experience" without dogma is very different from the experience of believing a dogma.' [7]

Four Quartets are his ripest, most complex and most complete expression of 'the experience of believing a dogma'; of the moments of intuitive apprehension of its truth, and of the relation of these to a view of history and to the general living of life. Of the 'mystical' experiences of the moments of vision, Eliot says in his essay on Pascal,[8] 'you may call it communion with the Divine, or you may call it a temporary crystallisation of the mind,' and he comments that such illuminations occur to many people who are not mystics, and that 'they can be judged only by their fruits.' *Four Quartets* are religious poems, but as Eliot said of other great religious

---

[7] 'Planning and Religion,' *Theology*. May 1943.

[8] The whole of this essay throws much light on the attitude of mind behind *Four Quartets*.

poetry, the poet is not persuading us to believe anything, he is revealing what it feels like to believe his religion. And to believe it not only intellectually, but with the whole personality. He is creating in language the steps in thought and feeling, and the moments of sudden apprehension, in and through which he has felt the conflicting oppositions of the worlds of nature and of 'spirit'; of time and the timeless; of the personal and the social; of inner and outer actualities; of life and death, to be 'conquered and reconciled' in the central symbol of Incarnation, although that remains only 'half-guessed, half understood.' Of how, moreover, the principle of incarnation seems to work on all sorts of levels, appearing in 'hints and guesses' in all those creative aspects of living by which humanity transcends, and always has transcended, its slavery to time and place.

Steps in the historical growth of this process of revelation are hinted at in the quotations from Heraclitus and the Bhagavad-gita, but what to Eliot is the ultimate revelation is never presented directly. It appears in allusion and quotation from Dante, from medieval English mystics, from St. John of the Cross, and in connecting the poems with events in the Church calendar, but never by direct quotation of the familiar, smooth-worn words of the Gospels. It is only by implication that we continually hear the old words in a new voice, and particularly those telling of the way, the truth, and the life. Nor is anything ever presented as the dogma of a Church. The full illumination of the Christian concept is not the starting point but what is *arrived* at. The poems are a process of exploration, both *along* the movements of time, and *inward* into the stillness of 'consciousness.' This idea emerges in the imagery of *travelling*, which is sustained throughout. What is arrived at, the moments of intensified living, are also subtly transformed, as the quality of revelation grows and spreads. And the two processes by which the truth is revealed—through the way and through the life—the travelling and the sense of arrival, the means and the ends, the becoming and the being, are inseparable, always in a condition of interpenetration and intertwining. The two modes of experiencing—by exploration and by apprehension—are again reflected in the ways in which the poet approaches his themes. The whole sequence opens with a passage of musing philosophical speculation and ends with a passage of the utmost symbolic intensity and concentration. The approach by way of analytical exploration, and the direct intuitive revelation through symbol alternate throughout, merge into one another by subtle transitions and become one in the total rhythmical structure.

A parallel between the living of life with its centre in the symbol of Incarnation, and the creation of art as another symbol of which incarnation is the centre, is sustained throughout. Poetry and music are united in the title of the poems.[9] The parallel between the creation of life and art will be discussed later, but the title is one illustration of the 'fourness' which Jung emphasizes so much as an element in the mandala pattern. This goes far beyond the musical suggestion and is of the greatest intricacy and elaboration. The whole design is of a four-in-one. The division of the physical universe into the four elements of air, earth, water and fire is used symbolically to express the elements in the nature of man which make him the microcosm of the macrocosm. His powers of abstraction are air; the chemical composition of his body is earth; the lifestream in his blood is water; his spirit is fire. Each poem emphasizes one element in particular. Each poem too creates one of four different ways of looking at time: time as memory; time as a cyclical pattern; time as flux; time as the revelation

---

[9] A parallel with musical structure is discussed by Helen L. Gardner in Four Quartets: A Commentary (*T. S. Eliot: A study of his writings by several hands*, pp. 58-60). The whole essay is full of valuable suggestions.

of the meaning of 'history.' Time itself is the fourth dimension of space. The title of each poem is the name of a place, and that place is related to the poet's experience in the present, and to events in the past. The four seasons play their part and are related to four periods in the life of man.

All these quarters which make the various 'quaternities' are enclosed within an image of human experience as 'the turning world.' But the image of the turning world is twofold: there are two co-existent turning worlds, two 'spheres of existence.' One is the physical, external world of temporal and spatial manifestations; the world of perpetual change. The other is the unseen world of inner unchanging pattern, whose centre is 'the still point.' Man is 'involved' with both and is part of the pattern of both. The themes of the poems are the revelation of this double relationship—to the world of nature and to the world of spirit—and of the results of the *lack* of relationship.

These themes have their first statements in the two epigraphs from Heraclitus. The first says: 'Although the Word (logos) is common to all, most men live as if they had each a private wisdom of his own.' The second says: 'The way up and the way down are one and the same.' Philip Wheelwright [10] explains the idea behind the second epigraph thus:

> 'The way up' meant to Heraclitus, outwardly, the qualitative movement from rock and earth through the intermediate stages of mud, water, cloud, air, and aether, to the rarest and uttermost of all states, which is fire; 'the way down' meant the contrary movement. Both the movements are in process all the time in all things that exist, hence they are said to be 'the same.' Existence thus involves unceasing tension between up-

[10] 'Eliot's Philosophical Themes.' *T. S. Eliot: A study of his writings by several hands*, p. 100.

ward and downward pulls—toward the realm of rarity, warmth, light and toward the realm of density, cold, dark. The pull is not only observed in physical phenomena, it operates too in our souls.

All things exist in tension, but to Heraclitus the 'reconciliation of the opposites' means their creative interdependence in accordance with a universal law but not their transcendence. He has no concept of a 'still point' where all the emotional oppositions are 'gathered and reconciled' and 'conquered' by having *meaning* in terms of resolution. So that Eliot's interpretation of 'the way up and the way down' is not that of Heraclitus. To him the words mean that an exploration of all the human emotional equivalents of birth-death, war-peace, day-night, height-depth, heat-cold, movement-stillness, leads to the discovery that all the 'ways' lead to the 'life' in the centre, and to the revelation of the 'truth' of that symbol. It is the revelation *in* 'the turning world' of 'the word which is common to all.'

Outside the turning worlds of human experience, both outer and inner, is the Logos itself, the 'unmoved mover':

> Love is itself unmoving,
> Only the cause and end of movement.

But that Absolute is unattainable since humanity is inextricably involved within the physical turning world where all time and movement are relative. The 'still point' therefore is *the point of intersection* between time and the timeless, between stillness and movement, and partakes of the qualities of both the eternal unmoving Logos and the inescapable world of time and movement: 'only through time time is conquered.' If we try to place it in definition, in time it is the 'eternal present,' the dimension of time existing outside its divisions into the cycle of past, present and future, but which has to be defined in temporal terms. If we try to define it in space, we have to envisage (to quote Mr. Wheelwright again) 'a mathematically pure point' existing at the centre of a revolving wheel: again not a part of its movement, but to be expressed only by reference to movement. For an inescapable condition of our physical turning world is that we exist in space-time.

But our punctual rotary prison, with physical dissolution as the inevitable and inexorable end of our sojourn in it, can be transformed if we become a part of the inner pattern, the other 'sphere of existence,' which, though unseen, inheres in it. We are made fully aware of it only in those moments of 'communion with the Divine' or of 'temporary crystallisation of the mind,' when the sense of 'wholeness' becomes an actuality. In those moments we reach 'the still point'; we are conscious of release from the tension of the opposites and their sudden resolution into harmony. 'Sudden in a shaft of sunlight' these moments of insight and intensification of living, come; and in those moments we touch 'reality.' They may occur in memory or day-dream; in religious contemplation; in any moment of 'sudden illumination,' and in the full experience of works of art. The rest is, from one point of view 'the waste, sad time stretching before and after.' But nevertheless that can be lived in the light of the revelation, in the knowledge that the pattern subsists. Though the individual is in the midst of the oppositions and conflicts, doomed to ego-consciousness, a part of the eternal flux, a unit in society, a fragment in history, a mere 'word' or 'note,' still the hidden design is there, 'in the world and for the world.' If the individual consciousness recognizes this, it has a centre towards which all action may point, round which it can revolve, and from which it is controlled. It will then 'move in measure like a dancer'; and at moments it will experience 'the still point' where the stillness and dancing become one.

The still point may be reached by the 'way' through any of the apparent opposites; through light or darkness, a beginning or an ending, harmony or silence, plenitude or vacancy, movement or abstention from movement. Any way will prove to be 'the same' and each to include the other, as part of the whole, in the 'sphere' whose centre is the point. But in absolute contrast to this patterned existence are all those uncoordinated oppositions and conflicts which are without a central control. In the individual life, there are the 'ways' which are, as it were, spokes in the wheel and all part of the design centreing in the 'mathematically pure point' at its axis. To follow these is to be a part of the larger pattern; to be within the 'dance.' But in absolute contrast to that is the confusion and *lack* of pattern if the only centre of existence is the ego; if life is lived 'as if each had a private wisdom of his own.' Then there is no co-ordinating pattern and the movements and stillnesses which result are of a completely different character.

In image after image Eliot suggests the quality of the passively inert or actively errant existence which is governed neither by the great ordered rhythms of the external world, nor by the inner order of the imaginary wheel. Such existence is to be neither in 'the way up' or 'the way down'; it is to be

> in a dark wood, in a bramble,
> On the edge of a grimpen, where is no secure foothold . . .

It is to be neither in the controlled rhythm of movement, nor the controlled 'stillness,' but to be 'that which is only moved/ And has in it no source of movement.' It is a condition of

> Tumid apathy with no concentration
> Men and bits of paper, whirled by the cold wind . . .

It is to be 'in a drifting boat with a slow leakage.' It is to be neither in active life nor in that creative 'death' which precedes rebirth, but to be in anaesthesia, when 'the mind is conscious, but conscious of nothing.' It is to be neither in day nor night, but a time that is 'dark in the afternoon.' It is neither attachment nor detachment, but 'indifference.' It is not harmony nor silence but a 'twittering world,' or among voices 'scolding, mocking or merely chattering.'

The great dramatic oppositions in the poems then, are between the way and the life of creative, organic order, and the way and the death of destructive inorganic disorder. It is in those terms that Good and Evil are presented: pattern and lack of pattern; design and chaos. The poems create a vision of the whole of human experience seen within this cosmic outline. That is their philosophic aim and end. But *Four Quartets* are poetry before they are philosophy, or at least the philosophy is inseparable from the poetry. It is in terms of the word as *mythos* that they create it as *logos*. It is precisely as Eliot said of Dante: 'The insistence throughout is upon states of feeling: the reasoning takes only its proper place as a means of reaching these states.'

BURNT NORTON

The title is the name of a manor house in Gloucestershire. Since in the other three poems the place-name of the title relates the poet himself to the particular theme of the poem, it seems likely that this does too. It may be the scene of a memory, or a place where the vision of a 'might have been' formed itself in his consciousness. But as I have said, besides bringing the associations of four different places, each of the poems is associated with one of the four elements, and the reflection of this element in the nature of man permeates the theme and is the starting point for its statement. In *Burnt Norton* the element is air, which corresponds as it were to the thought processes in man; his possession of memory, and his power of intellectual speculation and spiritual contemplation.

The poem opens with a passage of musing commentary on the nature of experience in time, with three self-contained propositions, and then a statement of what is really the substance and conclusion of all four poems.[11] First there is the usual concept of time as progression, and events as a sequence of cause and effect:

> Time present and time past
> Are both perhaps present in time future,
> And time future contained in time past.

Then there is the concept of time as 'eternally present,' with the comment that if that is so, it makes time 'unredeemable'; nothing can be altered, we can't bring back the past. This statement is left as it is for the moment: it is developed in the later poems and shown to be a half truth only. Finally there is a third category of experience 'what might have been'—the potential. This is 'perpetual,' but exists only 'in a world of speculation.' The three aspects of time are then reduced to the central truth:

> What might have been and what has been
> Point to one end, which is always present.

This is the first entrance of subtle ambiguity in the language, with its two-faced meanings of *point, end* and *present*. As a summing up of time as progression, it says that what has been (the past) and what might have been (the potentialities of the past) point to the present as their conclusion: that is what they have produced. As a summing up of the second idea of the eternal present as a 'point,' it says that what that points to is both that the present moment is the only actuality, and that what to do in the present is an *aim* or purpose which is always present with us.

Then the pure abstraction modulates into a transition passage. 'What might have been' is translated into the sensuous embodiment of the echoing footfalls down the imaginary pas-

---

[11] Though it is usual to refer to Bergson's theories of Time as Eliot's starting point, Louis L. Martz, in an interesting article in *The Sewanee Review* (Winter 1947: reprinted in *T. S. Eliot: A Selected Critique*), quotes passages from St. Augustine's *Confessions* which are very pertinent.

sage to the closed door into the rose-garden. 'My words echo /
Thus in your mind,' says the poet. He may be addressing the
reader and suggesting that such experiences are common to all;
or the echoes may be in the mind of the woman in the imaginary scene. Then he returns to the symbolic presentation of
the past as 'dust on a bowl of rose-leaves.' What *purpose* can
such disturbing memories have, since the past is unredeemable,
its pattern unalterable?

The rhythm quickens to a sense of breathless expectancy
and creates the sense of the mind darting about, confusing the
logic of temporal and spatial happenings in its own spontaneous
flight into 'the garden.' The interpretation of the lovely scene
in the rose-garden itself must depend on personal readings.
Many people seem to feel it as a memory of childhood, taking
'our first world' to mean that. I interpret the whole passage in
the light of the line between the conclusion of the development
of all the themes and the final recapitulation at the end of
Little Gidding: 'With the drawing of this Love and the voice
of this Calling.' That transfigures the bird and the roses of
Burnt Norton into the dove of *Little Gidding* and the rose of
fire and light at the end of that poem: that is, nature becomes
a symbol of a spiritual truth which transcends it. By the end
of the poems 'our first world' and the children in the leaves
hold a suggestion of the age of innocence in the Garden of
Eden, before the pattern of perfect relationship between God,
man and nature was clouded and darkened. Here, in *Burnt
Norton,* a transcendence of nature is brought about by the
experience being 'an airy nothing' given 'a local habitation,'
and by its fusion of nature and man into perfect inter-relationship. But the experience itself—that of *this* love and *this* calling—seems to me to be that of love as a part of the natural
world, the 'first world' of our development as human beings,
the first 'gate' on the way. The voice of the thrush is 'deception,' partly because the whole thing is unseen and unheard
by the outward senses, and partly because the experience,

though it is one of the moments of 'reality,' contains only a partial revelation of it, since its centre is in the sense world.

The vision is created in flowing, free and melodious rhythms, its invisible and inaudible quality mysteriously carried by the clearest pictures and verse music. The actual setting in place and time is an autumn scene, but the echoing footfalls of memory and might-have-been enter the deserted rose-garden and people it with life from an inner world. The voice of the bird calls in response to 'unheard music' in the shrubbery; the unseen figures *must* be there 'for the roses had the look of flowers that are looked at.' The roses (the emblems of earthly love) and the dream figures from the past are blended into an inseparable union of giving and receiving, 'accepted and accepting.' With that the scene groups itself round a symbolic centre 'in a formal pattern.' The roses and the figures move, concentrating the 'point' of vision from the garden to the evergreen 'box circle' and thence to the pool and the lotos. The actual deserted drained pool, and its emotional counterpart in the hardness and dryness and neutral shades of the actuality of life, are suddenly transformed into the exquisite moment:

> And the pool was filled with water out of sunlight,
> And the lotos rose, quietly, quietly,
> The surface glittered out of heart of light,
> And they were behind us, reflected in the pool.

Here in natural terms, in the autumn 'vibrant air' is the parallel with what in *Little Gidding* is the 'mid-winter spring' of the pentecostal fire, which is 'not in the scheme of generation.' Here, nature and man seem part of an indestructible unity and harmony which *is* within the scheme of generation; the golden cup of the lotos and the surface of the pool receiving their glittering light from the physical sun; the human figures and the roses reflected in the water; the fading leaves full of children 'hidden excitedly, containing laughter.' The vision is that of an ecstasy of fulfilment at the human and natural level, which is a beautiful 'reality,' though not the ultimate one. It is blotted out by the cloud, the bird says 'Go, go, go'—leave *that* garden—and we are brought back from the vision to the grave statement of the opening, that all things 'point to one end, which is always present.'

The lovely dancing lyric at the opening of the second movement is obviously based on the Heraclitean idea of the perpetual strife which resolves itself into beautiful harmony. The apparently conflicting and the apparently static are all part of an eternal moving pattern, existing simultaneously in all the elements in nature and linking them in a dynamic whole. The only inanimate thing is 'the bedded axle-tree,' maybe a relic of some chariot or gun-carriage in a 'forgotten war,' but reminding us of the symbol of the wheel.[12] From the bright stones under it and the bright flowers around it, from under the 'sodden floor' up to the stars, there streams up and down this uninterrupted energy of strife, forming itself into harmonious living patterns; singing, dancing, circulating, and having their final meaning in 'the stars,' the reflection of the Heraclitean 'fire.' Even the rather horrible strife of pursuer and pursued, the boarhound and the boar, is constellated (like the warring of the Olympian gods?) into an eternally subsisting order.

But then there is a complete change of rhythm. Heraclitus' system had no still point, which makes his dance very different. His concept of reconciliation is that of perpetual sustaining tension between opposites and not of a centre of resolution. How then define this centre dispassionately, rationally? In place of the crowding, swift images creating the ever-changing configurations of natural forces, the rhythm becomes slow, the

[12] In the light of the later Quartets, I suspect that the bedded axle tree may be a concealed symbol of Incarnation, and that the 'bedded' and 'tree' unite manger and cross. Nature with all her patterns *clots* our realisation of the spiritual pattern which is imbedded in nature and yet a different 'sphere.' But the image is not developed in the other poems and this may be forcing a meaning.

vocabulary abstract, the method analytical. But the poet finds the language of logic inadequate here. The still point can be approached only through paradox and negation. It is nothing that can be measured in terms of time, or of movement and fixity, of body or spirit, of ascent and descent. And yet it cannot be detached from these things, because though it is the point where there is no movement, it controls all the movement, and it is only through the measured movements that its presence can be known. It exists, but cannot be captured in a *where* or *when*.

Breaking off the effort at definition by negation and exclusion, the next sequence, continuing the analytical approach, describes in positive terms the *quality* of the experience, which has been given direct sensuous revelation in the vision in the rose-garden. It is a feeling of detachment from the ego and its conflicts, with a sense of grace and illumination and combined stillness and movement; a keeping of personal identity, and of the world of human experience, and yet an expansion beyond it and an elevation above it. Above all a sense of *wholeness*, in which the fragmentary nature of human experience, its partial ecstasy, and its partial horror, are completed and resolved and given *meaning*. Yet man, because he is human, cannot live at the level of the apprehension of wholeness. 'Woven in the weakness of the changing body' are the inextricable strands which chain him to time and change. But the chains protect him too. They protect him from more than glimpses of absolute good or evil, ecstasy or agony, 'which flesh cannot endure'—whose *duration* would cost man his humanity, since time and change are the laws of his being.[13] He has these moments of ecstasy when he seems to transcend time and conquer it, but it is only within the pattern of time that they can be seen to be a part of a timeless pattern.

[13] These lines recall the passage in the Bhagavad-gita where Krishna, at Arjuna's request, reveals himself in his divine Form. The glory and horror are so overwhelming that Arjuna cannot endure the revelation, and begs the God to resume his incarnation as friend and fellow-mortal.

The third movement introduces the theme which is in absolute contrast to that of life as part of an ordered natural process, and of life as a pattern of inner relationships centred in the still point, and pointed towards it. It is that of life with no centre, no ordered direction, no organic relationships. Eliot creates these antitheses into a passage where images of them and the language in which they are described produce the most immediate and concrete sensations. On the one hand we feel the true emotional oppositions, by any of which the still point may be reached and which are as patterned as the natural images which symbolize them; on the other all the confusion and fragmentariness and negative neutrality of the dim 'place of disaffection.' That word itself at once condenses a complex of ideas of the cause and effect of the condition. It carries connotations of discontent; of the diminution and alienation of affection; and of disorder. The next lines contrast the oppositions which are rendered *lucid* by the sense of pattern, with the disaffection and dimness, which are

> neither daylight
> Investing form with lucid stillness
> Turning shadow into transient beauty
> With slow rotation suggesting permanence
> Nor darkness to purify the soul
> Emptying the sensual with deprivation
> Cleansing affection from the temporal.
> Neither plenitude nor vacancy.

The London scene which follows continues the parallels. Instead of creative tension there is *strain* on the 'time-ridden faces / Distracted from distraction by distraction.' Instead of light or dark, a *flicker* and *faded air* and *gloomy hills;* instead of plenitude or vacancy, the faces 'filled with fancies and empty of meaning'; instead of wholeness, *unwholesome* lungs, *unhealthy* souls; instead of permanence and lucid stillness, the *tumid apathy* of the *torpid;* instead of measured movement the 'men and bits of paper, whirled by the cold wind.'

From all 'this twittering world' of dim light and dim humanity, the poet turns to the creative 'way down' into the inner
darkness and isolation and silence, to the vacancy which is
not 'empty of meaning,' but empty of self. It is 'deprivation /
And destitution of all property,' the active forsaking of the
ego, the way of withdrawal from the worlds of both sense and
spirit, the disciplined 'abstention from movement';

>   while the world moves
>   In appetency, on its metalled ways
>   Of time past and time future.

Here again in *appetency* there is a great concentration of meaning. Not only the sense of conscious and unconscious compulsive drives, but the reminder of the Lamarckian doctrine that
changes in the desires and needs of an organism result in
adaptive modifications of its structure. So that the 'metalled
ways' on which the urban world now moves, suggest not only
a picture of it as a vast network of roads and railways leading
nowhere, but the whole quality of the mechanistic culture of
today and its possible consequences for the future of the race.

After the formal declaration and loaded latinized language
of the third movement, the short lyric of the fourth takes us
back to the memory of the vision in the garden, but in a very
different mood. There, there was the ecstatic assurance of lucid
pattern uniting nature and man. This was reinforced by the
lyric emphasizing the dynamic order of the natural world and
the passages of analysis describing the order of the world of
spirit. Against this was the disorder of the modern city. From
this the poet turned to a discipline of spiritual negation and a
conquest of sense. But that is a voluntary darkness and emptiness; there is a return from it to the world which had been
renounced. What of the involuntary defeat of the darkness and
silence of death, which is the inevitable end of 'the changing

body?' With mingled horror and hope the poet questions its meaning.

> Time and the bell have buried the day,
> The black cloud carries the sun away.

The day and all that daylight brought, 'investing form with lucid stillness' and the sense of permanent moving pattern, is 'buried'; its lucid stillness destroyed by the black cloud and the death knell. The only sense of movement is the carrying away of the sun by the cloud, not only obscuring but *removing* the unmoving centre of the universe as we know it. This fact brings at one level sensations of pure terror. The words *bury, cloud, clutch, cling, curled fingers,* and the isolation of *chill* as a line in itself, suggest obliteration, dark cold extinction, strangulation by forces against which man is helpless. Will the only centre of life then be the nourishment our rotting bodies supply to the loveliness of flowers and trees? But there is another tone of gentler questioning. To pass into the pattern of nature expressed in the turning of the sunflower; in the tendrils and sprays of the clematis straying down, bending, clutching and clinging; in the curled fingers of the yew, has its own beauty. But will it be all? The tones of both horror and tender regret in the question are answered by the flashing image of the kingfisher in relation to the source of natural light, and its parallel in terms of the spirit.

> After the kingfisher's wing
> Has answered light to light, and is silent, the light is
>   still
> At the still point of the turning world.

The opposition of the movement of the kingfisher's wing and silence, in the last image, leads on to the next subject, the union of movement and stillness in a work of art and its parallel with the worlds of time and the still point. The poet shifts again to analytical discourse, this time in flowing speech rhythms. Again we have the two worlds of the temporal and the unchanging contrasted. The actuality of poetry and music to eye and ear is a series of progressions in a temporal sequence. But if they existed only in that dimension they would die like the flower and the kingfisher. Their 'reality' is a matter of dynamic relationships, a structure where every part is involved with every other part to form an indivisible whole. The temporal sequence is co-existent with the unchanging pattern, all held together in a vital tension of sound and meaning. Carrying on the image of the whole as a system of tensions, he says:

> Words strain,
> Crack and sometimes break, under the burden,
> Under the tension, slip, slide, perish,
> Decay with imprecision, will not stay in place,
> Will not stay still. Shrieking voices
> Scolding, mocking, or merely chattering,
> Always assail them.

We shift almost imperceptibly from the abstract discussion of an intellectual aesthetic to the immediate reminder that this is by way of illustration of something else. The theme is not primarily a matter of aesthetics or physics. The *burden* is not only the weight on a word. The *imprecision* is linked with the concrete *decay*, the loss of tension with the concrete *slip, slide, perish*. The abstract stillness and movement of poetic 'form' is invaded by the discordant, irrelevant 'voices.' In the last image the sense of *dis*order is suddenly intensified and its menace as the enemy of pattern and permanence is created in the word *assail*. Then 'words' become the Word and we are translated from art to life.

> The Word in the desert
> Is most attacked by voices of temptation,
> The crying shadow in the funeral dance,
> The loud lament of the disconsolate chimera.

The temptation, the *attack* on creative order, becomes the wonderful complex imagery of the last two lines, where the harmonious dance is disturbed by 'the funeral dance,' and where noise, darkness, self-pity and self-deception invade the stillness. 'The disconsolate chimera' is another of those strokes of genius where the words absorb and radiate implications. *Disconsolate,* recalling the earlier *disaffection,* carries the meaning of comfortless and melancholy, while *chimera* is both an empty, meaningless fancy and the incongruously composed monster slain by Bellerophon. Every aspect of the meanings fuse, and the *loud lament* and the *crying shadow* again enforce the sense of discord, pain and confused darkness of the temptation.

The recapitulation of the whole poem moves in a measure of short fluent lines, which is used again at the conclusion of *The Dry Salvages* and *Little Gidding.* The pattern of dynamic tensions sustaining life, which in the natural world was 'figured in the drift of stars' and down to the garlic and the mud, is, in the world of spirit 'the figure of the ten stairs.' This is a reference to St. John of the Cross, who pictured the discipline of contemplation as a ladder of ten steps 'which the soul is ascending and descending continually in ecstasy and humiliation until it has acquired perfect habits.' The summit of the ladder and what it rests upon is God as Love, and for a moment we are taken outside of both the turning world and the pattern whose centre is the still point, to the unmoved mover who exists untouched by the temporal, by the 'form of limitation' decreed by life. Love in its human aspect cannot rid itself entirely of the element of desire. It can reach only to the moment of 'reality' in the rose-garden, when, for a brief instant, nature and spirit glittered together 'out of heart of light.' Swiftly we are transported back to that ecstasy—

> Sudden in a shaft of sunlight
> Even while the dust moves

> There rises the hidden laughter
> Of children in the foliage
> Quick now, here, now, always—

The 'purpose' of the disturbance of the dust on the bowl of rose-leaves is now clear. It is a reminder that every moment of time can be transfigured by the apprehension of the timeless pattern and the sharing of its vitality. The release, the 'grace of sense,' the spontaneous, joyous illumination, comes like the 'dancing arrow' [14] of bird flight, flashes in the here and now— and is gone—leaving the sense of the combined unimportance and unworthiness and mockery of 'the aspect of time.'

> Ridiculous the waste sad time
> Stretching before and after.

EAST COKER

In *East Coker*,[15] although, as in all the Quartets, the themes are the same, they are felt in a completely different emotional context and treated in a completely different mood of response. Instead of the philosophical abstraction and objective detachment of *Burnt Norton,* there is direct personal application. It is the most openly personal poem Eliot has ever written, though it is characteristic that he is not being personal about a purely private experience. He speaks as an individual member of a society totally involved in the same problem. The prose statement of the position is in a passage of *The Idea of a Christian Society,* published in 1939, the year before the publication of the poem.

[14] See the short poem *Cape Ann.*

[15] J. J. Sweeney was the first critic to identify the allusions in the poem and to elucidate its structure. (*Southern Review*—Spring 1941) I am particularly indebted to his essay, which is now reprinted in *T. S. Eliot: A Selected Critique.*

I believe that there must be many persons who, like
myself, were deeply shaken by the events of September 1938; persons to whom that month brought a pro-
founder realization of a general plight . . . a feeling of
humiliation which seemed to demand an act of personal
contrition, of humility, repentance and amendment; a
doubt of the validity of a civilization . . . Was our
society, which had always been so assured of its superiority and rectitude, so confident of its unexamined
premises, assembled round anything more permanent
than a congeries of banks, insurance companies, and
industries, and had it any beliefs more essential than a
belief in compound interest and the maintenance of
dividends?

It is this situation, within the framework of the larger pattern, which the poem creates. From this identification of himself with the society of which he is inescapably a part, come
the passages of uncompromising denunciation of that society,
and of ruthless self-examination and self-dissection. From that
too comes the sense of stifling oppression and failure and
fatigue which colours most of the poem and is dispersed only
at its conclusion.

The element in the natural world which has its reflection in
the nature of man is here *earth*. Man is a part of the processes
of nature. He is not only involved in time as an abstract progression of past, present, future, but in the cyclical pattern of
its practical aspect as birth, maturity, decay, death. This is the
pattern woven in his changing body, and it is the pattern of
the works of his hands and of his mind; of his houses, his political ideas, his social structures. This is the link with the place-
name. Coker is a small village in Somersetshire, which was the
reputed birthplace of Sir Thomas Elyot, who in 1531 published
The Boke named the Gouvenour. The book is one of those
treatises on new moral, political educational and literary ideals,
which were the result of the 'revival of learning' and the fresh

interest in the study of the classics. It was inspired by all the hopes of the dawn of a new era; of a Renaissance from the Dark Ages. Eliot himself, from the birthplace of his ancestors, from the darkness of a new dark age, from a personal darkening of the spirit, surveys past, present and personal.

The poem opens with the assertion of what had been speculation at the opening of *Burnt Norton*. 'Perhaps,' said the poet there, perhaps present and past are both present in the future. But now we are presented with the concrete, indubitable facts of life in the sequence of time. They are determined by the unalterable laws by which an end succeeds a beginning, by which the only unending thing is change, and by which dust returns to dust and man's body becomes finally part of the chemical composition of the soil itself.

In the last section of *Burnt Norton,* where the first reference was made to beginnings and endings, they were shown to be necessary but 'unreal' aspects of a work of art, which truly exists in the form and pattern. That is a whole, just as the eternal metaphysical 'reality' is a whole, to which any point in the temporal or spatial order is equally relevant. But the opening of *East Coker* insists upon life as 'succession.' In the same way, 'the way up and the way down' in nature are seen here not as creative tensions but as successive 'rising and falling' in a ceaseless process of change.

> Old stone to new building, old timber to new fires,
> Old fires to ashes, and ashes to the earth
> Which is already flesh, fur and faeces,
> Bone of man and beast, cornstalk and leaf.

There is the life-rhythm which is that of 'generation': [16]

---

[16] Cf: *Ecclesiastes III*. There are verbal echoes from this chapter throughout the poem and Eliot obviously intends us to have it in mind.

> there is a time for building
> And a time for living and for generation
> And a time for the wind to break the loosened pane
> And to shake the wainscot where the field-mouse trots
> And to shake the tattered arras woven with a silent
> motto.

This is the rhythm of succession (and . . . and . . . and). The movement is that of the 'trot' of the mouse, and of the wind of time that shakes and breaks. The only stillness is that of the dead house and the silent motto.[17]

With the repetition of the opening words in the next paragraph the focus shifts from the general statement, created in all its particularity of image, to the scene in the immediate present, the 'now.' Here, although the whole flavour of the poetry is so different, we are back in the same quality of civilization created in the London scene in *Burnt Norton*. Again there is the same half-light and half-life: nothing is clear. There is light in the open field, but the deep lane 'where you lean against a bank while a van passes' is 'shuttered with branches, dark in the afternoon':

> in a warm haze the sultry light
> Is absorbed, not refracted, by grey stone.

It is not the 'lucid stillness, turning shadow into transient beauty.' It has no radiance; it reflects back nothing from its source. There is an absolute contrast with the scene in the rose-garden. There it was autumn too, but the air was 'vibrant'

---

[17] The silent motto has been identified with that of Mary, Queen of Scots, *En ma fin est mon commencement*. While this is helpful in some ways, I feel myself that it distracts attention from the imaginary decayed manor house of Coker, where that would not be the motto. In some notes sent by Eliot to his late brother Henry, which Mrs. Theresa Eliot has kindly allowed me to see, the comment on the words is: 'Eliot motto *tace et fac*.' 'Be silent and act' could be interpreted as the same as 'We must be still and still moving.'

in the heat, and the birds and the roses and the human figures partook of a shared vitality in the sunlight. Here 'in the electric heat / Hypnotised,' there is no vitality:

> The dahlias sleep in the empty silence.
> Wait for the early owl.

The flowers share the same quality as the light and the empty silence: everything is in a state of suspended animation, waiting for the ominous hoot of the owl and the coming of night. But 'the deep lane insists on the direction / Into the village'; it points there as the beginning, for this is the afternoon of the dawn dreamed of by Sir Thomas Elyot as the opening of a new era.

What has now become a deep lane was then an open field, and 'if you do not come too close,' if you will distance it all into a vision, you will see the essentials of Sir Thomas's dream in a picture of country dancers round a bonfire on a summer night. The music of 'the weak pipe and the little drum' is very far away, but the dream had a real beauty. It was of man as an inseparable part of the rhythm of the natural world, and of his dancing as a symbol of 'sondry vertues,' particularly the ideas of pattern, harmony and 'concorde.' 'And for as moche as by the association of a man and a woman in daunsing may be signified matrimonie, I could in declarynge the dignitie and commoditie of that sacrament make intiere volumes.' Eliot has condensed the last seven words into the happy phrase 'commodious sacrament,' and he has made Elyot's commentary into a most delightful Breughelesque scene. But in spite of the 'sondry vertues' in the rhythm of this dancing, and its contrast to the men and bits of paper whirled by the cold wind, it is not the dancing at the still point. It is the rhythm of inexorable succession,

> Feet rising and falling.
> Eating and drinking. Dung and death.

In the little finale to the movement this is again emphasized. The sea image weaves several suggestions in its simple lines. Dawn, the *point du jour,* silently points the facts of the cyclic recurrence of day and night, and points to the present atmosphere of heat and silence. The dawn wind 'wrinkles and slides,' bringing hints of old age, and the memory of the words that 'slip, slide, perish.' The poet is equally a part of the time cycle: he cannot escape from his historical setting and from the past which begat it.

The scene of the next lyric contrasts not only with the rustic life which kept the rhythm of 'the time of the seasons and the constellations,' but with that in *Burnt Norton* where all the patterns of the universe were 'reconciled among the stars.' Here is no reconciliation but only conflict and 'disturbance' and inextricable confusion: perpetual strife which produces no harmony. Instead of a temporal pattern of orderly creative sequence, or a spatial one of dynamic tensions, the 'creatures' of the universe are in a chaos of derangement and commotion, whose end can be only the final annihilation of life. Instead of being part of a 'slow rotation suggesting permanence,' they are

> Whirled in a vortex that shall bring
> The world to that destructive fire
> Which burns before the ice-cap reigns.

The poet then considers his poem, with its neo-classical decoration and its translation of human situation into analogies from nature, and decides that it is 'not very satisfactory.' Instead he ponders on the problem in the language of argument. But just as it is the particularity of each image which creates the inner, ordered life of the lyric, so it is the particularity in the use of *word* which creates the inner, ordered life of the argument. What did the dawn of the Renaissance expect its serene autumn to be? What was to be the ripe harvest of value in humanistic wisdom?

> Had they deceived us
> Or deceived themselves, the quiet-voiced elders,
> Bequeathing us merely a receipt for deceit?

As always when Eliot is reiterating and playing upon a word, we may be sure that he is 'squeezing' it to extract its full juice of meaning. In the lyric it is the loss of pattern which all the images have illustrated, and when he returns to metaphor at the end of this passage it is to that of losing the way on a journey. This is the clue to the five-times use of *deceive* within a few lines. To deceive is to lead into error: it is 'any disposition or practice which misleads another or causes him to believe what is false.' Hence the 'deceit' which we *received from* the quiet-voiced elders in the way of a *recipe* for living, reveals its falseness. That calm, clear, bright 'serenity' reveals itself as a 'deliberate' (hesitating) dullness or bluntness of sensitivity. With rising intensity, the lines restate what Eliot had said before in *Gerontion,* that history *in itself* is meaningless, its 'progress' illusory. 'The knowledge derived from experience' imposes a pattern from the past which inevitably falsifies. It falsifies because the Heraclitean saying is true that no man ever steps twice into the same stream, since both stream and man are part of the endless flux. But also falsifies because, seen in terms of the eternal pattern, every moment of human experience falls short.

> And every moment is a new and shocking
> Valuation of all we have been.

The errors which have already been detected by the advancement of empirical knowledge would in any case no longer lead us astray. Detection is not wisdom. And with superb irony the next passage points to that fact by bringing together Dante and Sherlock Holmes.

In the middle, not only in the middle of the way
But all the way, in a dark wood, in a bramble,
On the edge of a grimpen, where is no secure foothold,
And menaced by monsters, fancy lights,
Risking enchantment.

The opening of *The Divine Comedy:* 'In the middle of the journey of our life, I found myself in a dark wood, having lost the straight path,' is blended with the dark Grimpen Mire and the phosphorous-daubed face of the Hound of the Baskervilles. There is a memory too of the chimera of *Burnt Norton,* as well as of the fireflies which confused the detectives and the superstitious fears which falsified the problem. A hint too, I think, in the word *enchantment,* of the atmosphere of hypnosis suggested in the way and the day which is 'dark in the afternoon.'

The movement ends with the summing up of the lack of value in the mere acquisition of knowledge or in supposing that wisdom is cumulative either in the life of the individual or in that of society. To the poet, the central doctrine of Humanism, the autonomy of the individual spirit, is not wisdom but folly. The individual is not the ultimate Gouvernour, and he sees humanistic ideals as leading to spiritual pride and finally to the isolation of the individual in the prison of self. Wisdom and humility are two of the fruitful oppositions which prove to be 'the same' and are therefore endless. In the time-cycle the only endless thing is change, and the poet points to that in the last two lines. In that cycle man and the works of his hands, however worthy, are absorbed into the natural elements, earth and sea.

Into the atmosphere of the dark wood and the deep lane and the empty silence waiting for the early owl breaks a voice of prophetic denunciation. It denounces the deadness, darkness, blindness, vacancy, forlornness, in which, with chilled sense-perceptions and rational faculties, and the loss of any directed 'motive,' modern civilization is going to its death—a blind Samson without the inner vision which came to Milton's hero. The reiterated *vacant* brings first, in 'the vacant interstellar spaces,' the sense of the loss of relationship with the ordered living which 'kept time' with the seasons and the constellations; and further the remembrance of the 'vacant of meaning' in the Dantesque London scene in *Burnt Norton*. The pattern is obliterated. The only idea of an almanac, reminding us of the movements of the heavenly bodies, is a social register of rank: the only kind of Gouvernour or Director is that of a financial company. Hence there is no 'sense' or meaning or message in the oppositions of life and death. The funeral will be 'silent,' and the darkness is not that of 'destitution of property,' the renunciation of the personal as a 'motive of action': it is simply vacant lack of identity, 'there is no one to bury.'

From this outer directionless darkness, as from the similar scene in *Burnt Norton*, the poet turns inward to the chosen empty darkness of religious contemplation. In a transition passage of three elaborate similes, he compares it to the transference from one kind of darkness and emptiness to another within this dark modern existence. The movement of the verse is very heavy and perhaps the irony is on the heavy side too. Then the creative darkness and waiting and 'vacancy' are described, and the renunciation of the 'echoed ecstasy' which they demand.

> Whisper of running streams, and winter lightning.
> The wild thyme unseen and the wild strawberry,
> The laughter in the garden. . . .

Each image here suggests all the fresh sensuous delight which is utterly lacking to the cold senses of the modern social figures, or in the hypnosis and haze of the 'electric heat' of the dark afternoon. The whole rose-garden scene and its pattern is evoked, with the recognition that its 'reality' involves its opposite. The ecstasy is 'Not lost, but requiring, pointing to the agony / Of death and birth.' The ecstasy *requires* the agony, that is, it exacts it, and also, paradoxically, it *requests* it. The paradox is pointed to and resolved in the next lyric.

Hammering in the pointed requirement in the following passage, Eliot puts it largely in the actual words of St. John of the Cross; but with overtones of his own which take us back to *Burnt Norton* as well as to the first part of this movement. 'To arrive where you *are,* to get from where you *are not,*' is to achieve *consciousness,* or as much of it as can be achieved in time, in contrast to the anaesthesia and nonentity of 'the vacant.' And 'where you *are* is where *you* are not' points to the truth that the fullest consciousness is reached by the fullest renunciation of the personal.

The lyric fourth movement in *Burnt Norton* spoke of bodily death as part of a larger pattern: this Good Friday poem speaks of the spiritual death which is part of the pattern of redemption. It is in the tone and colouring of most of *East Coker,* as uncompromising and severe in its ethical content as it is strict in its stanzaic form and the working out of its metaphysical imagery and paradox. The central metaphor of the hospital may have been suggested by Sir Thomas Browne: 'For this world I count it not an Inn but an Hospital; a place not to live, but to dye in.' There is also a reference to St. John of the Cross, who speaks of the soul as 'under medical treatment for the recovery of its health, which is God himself.' The soul will be pierced 'with a dart of most enkindled love,' yet 'amidst these gloomy and loving pains, is conscious of a certain companionship and inward strength which attends upon it.' But Eliot's poem supports itself without need of outside sources to elucidate it, and he purposely avoids religious terminology. The lyric is an organic part of the rest of the poem, not a detached interpolation of a different nature from the rest. It is merely 'a new and shocking valuation' of what has gone before.

The 'earth' now becomes the nature of man, envisaged as a hospital, endowed by Adam, 'the ruined millionaire,' with original sin. Man in his folly likes to think he is 'substantial flesh and blood,' an autonomous entity in himself. Instead, his earthy body with its 'mental wires' is a suffering patient and his only health (wholeness) is in recognizing his 'disease,' his individual share in Adam's curse of being dust that will return to dust. That is the entire human condition; even the Church, the directing, mediating power is 'the dying nurse.' But within this inescapable mortal time-cycle, there is another cycle of death and rebirth; that of the human spirit. The 'absolute paternal care,' ever-present, 'prevents' us, that is both checks and guides, showing the way to do and be 'well,' the way towards 'health' through our dis-ease, our earthly suffering and voluntary death. We are each a 'distempered part,' a disordered fragment of the absolute wholeness. Our spiritual distemper reveals itself as a 'fever chart,' a confused series of 'rising and falling,' showing unresolved oppositions of temperature. This is the condition created already in terms of nature in the lyric at the opening of the second movement.

Always keeping within these controlling metaphors of the part and the whole; sickness and health; heat and cold; and 'up and down,' Eliot points to the resolution and reconciliation of these opposites. The wounded surgeon is a fellow man in the hospital, involved in its pain and suffering, while uniting that with 'absolute care' of the patients. There are no anaesthetics in this hospital, but the quality of the treatment which 'resolves the enigma of the fever chart' is created in the language used to describe it. The pointed steel is in itself piercing and merciless, but 'plies' introduces the idea of the pliant hands which enfold it; 'questions' brings the idea of tenderness and patience as well as stern examination, and 'sharp compassion' is the central emotional paradox of the healing and resolving. The bleeding hands direct the disordered rising and falling of the

fever chart into the pattern of 'the way up and the way down.'
Here it is the way down through the 'frigid purgatorial fires.'
Yet this fire is not 'that destructive fire / Which burns before
the ice-cap reigns.' It is creative, and it unites nature and
spirit, 'the flame is roses and the smoke is briars.' Its light is
the emblem of love; its dark not 'bramble' but a crown of
thorns. Light and dark do not follow one another in a time-
sequence, they are together, like the roses and the thorns. And
the destructive fire is not a prelude to an age of ice, the frigid
fires will become fused into warmth.

This movement of the opposites towards union and reconciliation is present throughout. Everything in the experience
reflects back to the paradox of the 'sharp compassion,' and
to the precise meaning of compassion. That suffering *with* is
the means of redemption, and is commemorated in that union
and communion in which the 'eating and drinking' of the
natural man become a sacramental symbol of a consubstantia-
tion.

The Good Friday symbol is the still point reached by the
way down through the darkness, with the revelation that there
descent and ascent, light and dark, death and rebirth, agony
and triumph, flesh and spirit, become one. And the 'beginning'
in Adam's fall has an end which is at the same time a beginning.
The conclusion of the poem finds a hope for men in the fact
that, in spite of their lack of humility, they have christened this
day 'good.'

It is in keeping with the whole atmosphere of *East Coker*
that Eliot follows this miraculously intricate piece of poetic
art and craft with a passage of the harshest self-criticism. In
relaxed, colloquial speech-verse he examines his own accomplishment as poet, his own 'way,' in itself, and as a part of the
tradition. For him too, as poet, there is 'only a limited value /
In the knowledge derived from experience.' Any imposed pat-

tern falsifies, and the vision of a perfect pattern in which words and music 'reach the stillness' is forgotten here. It is the sense of struggle which colours everything; 'the intolerable wrestle' between the poet and his medium. Every poem is 'a raid on the inarticulate,' that is an attack and invasion of an 'empty silence' where is neither speech nor movement. In tones of despair he sees himself,

> With shabby equipment always deteriorating
> In the general mess of imprecision of feeling,
> Undisciplined squads of emotion.

It is again characteristic that the enemy is not only the negative 'inarticulate' but the positive 'mess,' the emotional disorder. Conquest comes only through discipline. But there is also the temptation to think of poetry as a competition among poets and to despair on that ground. Again the answer is humility; an active humility requiring both strength and submission: a fight which is also a dedication. As he says in his essay on F. H. Bradley: 'We fight to keep something alive rather than in expectation that anything will triumph.' By the end of the passage the ground of the fight is shifting itself from that of 'trying to learn to use words' to the whole field of human endeavour.

The finale grows from this transition. The poet starts from the tradition as he finds it, and the achievements of other poets are not isolated 'intense moments' in a sequence of history. They become part of the poet's own struggle, ever alive in his medium, reminding him that the past is not just left behind, neither does it live only in the memory of its mistakes and failures. This thought gives a meaning to the intense moment which it did not have in *Burnt Norton*. It does not have meaning only as a release from individual tensions and a momentary sense of enhanced living, nor is it isolated in the waste sad time stretching before and after. It has the power to irradiate all life and time, as in the moment commemorated in Good

Friday. And in the historical terms of time, the living tradition, always being lost and found again, and the story of man's struggle, stretching back to 'old stones that cannot be deciphered,' unite all humanity in a sense of unity and continuity. The past is living as well as dead; its light is not absorbed but refracted. The inner life must be lived in the light of this. There is a sense of a half-emerging revelation here, which is held in suspension, because there is a great sense or urgency *forward* in his line of thought. There is a time for thinking of those who have added to one's own 'burning,' and to turn the pages of man's family album. But he reminds himself that his present task is a detachment from 'here and now' not in memories of the past, by a journey backwards in time, but by a journey inward into 'another intensity.' 'Old men ought to be explorers.' Tennyson's Ulysses thought so too: ('A perfect poem at that,' Eliot said of it). There too 'the deep moans round with many voices.' But this poet's exploration now is neither forward nor backward in time or place, 'here and there does not matter.' It is into the intensity of 'a further union, a deeper communion' with the spiritual subject of the Good Friday lyric; expressed in the depth and grandeur, the sadness and hope of the concluding rhythms.

> Through the dark cold and the empty desolation,
> The wave cry, the wind cry, the vast waters
> Of the petrel and the porpoise. In my end is my
>   beginning.

During the time span of the poem the poet has experienced a series of feelings of humiliation. First the humiliation of the law of the natural world that the human body will return to the earth 'which is already flesh, fur and faeces.' Then the humiliation of belonging to a decaying culture which is going into the dark. The bright dawn of the Renaissance has ended in the dark afternoon of the present. In the same way his own work appears a series of futile beginnings and endings with no real advance. The contemplation of the orderly seasons of nature, the disorderly courses of men, and the works of men's hands seems to lead equally to darkness, to a sense of despair. He turns from it all to allow the darkness of God to come upon him and to wait in complete stillness. The revelation which comes is of the 'reality' of the wounded surgeon, of the compassion and communion, and of the active life in time which brought redemption. From this he turns to his own form of communication, its own particular agonies, and the dedication to the 'trying.' This, though it demands endless humility and submission, has to be an active 'strength.' Turning again to the spiritual reality in the living of life, it translates itself into 'we must be still and still moving . . .' and is gathered up in the concluding images. But there the spiritual voyage is created in a metaphor from the world of nature, and though it is inward it is also forward through the living world and through time. The bitter sense of humiliation and despair has melted into one of a new humility of faith and love and hope, from which he is to start again, and out of which he can say: 'In my end is my beginning.' The way is still dark, but again the image is of a voyage *through* the night as well as in it. There is movement as well as stillness, and there is a time and a place where the darkness turns to light. And so, though no dawn points, he calls this Coker east.

THE DRY SALVAGES

The first and second Quartets have created the concepts of time first in the emblem of air, paralleled in human life as man's thought; and then in the emblem of earth, paralleled in human life as biological progression, and in history as a cyclic pattern of the birth, decay and death of human cultures. In *The Dry Salvages* the emblem of time is water, appearing in human life as the river of racial experience which runs in man's blood, and the sea of the vast flux of time on which he is afloat, and the life-element itself from which he developed. The poet's own experience flows into the poem through the identification of the river with the Mississippi, and the rocks and sea with the New England coast. But the tone changes from that of purposely personal introspection to that where the poet is the individual interpreter of general human experience.

It opens with a confession of ignorance as to how gods came into man's imagination, and then an imaging of racial history and its vitality both as river and as 'strong brown god.' The double metaphor is intertwined, some of the statements being in one part of it, some in the other. As river, racial history is first the crossing of the frontier between animal and human; then a matter of establishing practical trade relationships; finally of the development of all forms of communication. As god, it has both good and bad qualities. The danger is that men, having engineered by their own ingenuity all the transitions from pre-history to contemporary urban civilization, 'choose to forget' the god. He remains, though, the implacable destroyer, 'watching and waiting.' Man cannot dissociate himself from the bloodstream of his primitive ancestry, any more than from the seasonal time-cycle; and though the words are cunningly confused in the last four lines, we are made aware that the rank smell of the savage is present in our most polite circles.

While this river is within us, the tossing sea of human experience and the mingled beauty and terror of the elemental life-force in all its immeasurable flux is all about us. Eliot creates the one in terms of the other in the most powerful and exciting passage of description in the poems. 'The sea is the land's edge also,' the life-element merges with human experience of it. We can isolate bits of it for study, and so trace the course of evolution and the science of living organisms. But it flings at us reminders of how unequal is the struggle. 'It tosses up our losses,' illustrations of the futile attempts to catch it with nets and guide it with oars and master it with dead 'gear' foreign to its own nature. Its rhythms are far more powerful and varied than that of the river god within us. Human nature is only a part of the whole life-surge.

The verse rhythm pauses there for a moment, with the simple musical phrases uniting sea and land, 'menace and caress':

> The salt is on the briar rose,
> The fog is in the fir trees.

Then it deepens and sweeps in one sentence to the end of the movement, first creating life and time in images of sound.

>   The sea howl
> And the sea yelp, are different voices
> Often together heard; the whine in the rigging,
> The menace and caress of wave that breaks on water,
> The distant rote in the granite teeth,
> And the wailing warning from the approaching headland
> Are all sea voices, and the heaving groaner
> Rounded homeward, and the seagull:

Into this medley of sea sounds, on the surface of time as it were, there breaks another sound——

> And under the oppression of the silent fog
> The tolling bell
> Measures time not our time, rung by the unhurried
> Ground swell . . .

On the natural level the bell announces the presence of the eternal life-rhythms of the universe, 'watching and waiting,' to which the mere human seems petty and irrelevant. They are

> Older than the time of chronometers, older
> Than time counted by anxious worried women
> Lying awake, calculating the future,
> Trying to unweave, unwind, unravel

And piece together the past and the future,
Between midnight and dawn, when the past is all
  deception,
The future futureless, before the morning watch
When time stops and time is never ending;
And the ground swell, that is and was from the
  beginning,
Clangs
The bell.

In the image of the women Eliot manages to make us experience all those sensations of fragmentariness, misdirection, disorder and confusion which were present in the parallel suggestions in the earlier Quartets. But here there is a more purely human note, 'a deeper communion' with life-torn humanity spending its time in such futile calculations. From them, with the life-span of the individual represented as the pause of a comma, it passes to the morning watch in the final context,[18] and the eternal ground swell clangs its death-knell.

The sestina, with its slow rhythmic ground swell and subdued melancholy harmonies, pictures man's condition as that of being in a boat at sea: and all at sea in the colloquial connotation too. This voyage on the sea has the same qualities as that through the historical span in *East Coker*. The lifeless stillness and lifeless movement become

  The silent withering of autumn flowers
  Dropping their petals and remaining motionless

Men are pieces of 'drifting wreckage.' The command to watch and pray, because of the coming of death, hinted at in the lines before, cannot be heard. 'The prayer of the bone on the beach' is 'unprayable' just as there was no one to bury at the silent funeral. Where there is no faith in a purpose there can be no

[18] *Mark* XIII: 33-37.

help in prayer. And there is no aim or end to this drifting through time, only 'addition':

> the trailing
> Consequence of further days and hours,

sequence with no relation to anything outside itself. Instead of the active emotion of renunciation, feeling becomes mere increasing disillusionment about the brittleness 'of what was believed in as the most reliable.' The 'final addition' and what it all adds up to, is the picture of futile old age, with 'the unattached devotion which might pass for devotionless.' But though this may seem like true 'detachment,' it is only an apathetic resignation, a negative clinging to life, not to any value in life:

> In a drifting boat with a slow leakage,
> The silent listening to the undeniable
> Clamour of the bell of the last annunciation.

The fishermen in the next stanzas parallel the country dancers in *East Coker*. Their life does have a rhythm and an aim. It is active effort not passive drifting. But it is time-wrecked too, a part of the endless flux.

> There is no end of it, the voiceless wailing,
> No end to the withering of withered flowers,
> To the movement of pain that is painless and motion-
>   less,
> To the drift of the sea and the drifting wreckage,
> The bone's prayer to Death its God.

Death is absolute lord over life in time; and looking at that vast ocean, the power of individual man shrinks to that of a bare bone on the beach. And then, in the middle of the line, there is the sudden transition to the pattern where birth not death becomes the centre; creation not destruction.

> Only the hardly, barely prayable
> Prayer of the one Annunciation.

Mary's words at the Annunciation were 'Be it unto me according to thy word,' which is not an easy prayer for the Christian, but holds the hope of the miraculous birth promised by the angel.

After the drifting musical rise and fall of the sestina and its quiet whispering conclusion, the same subject is discussed analytically. What *is* permanent in this endless flux? There is a pattern of sequence, of addition, but no development. Any superficial or popular doctrine of evolutionary progress is a *partial fallacy*. All Eliot's dislike of such doctrine is in the words. It mistakes a part for the whole; it flatters man's conceit of himself; it fails to satisfy the conditions of logical proof; it is a deception and hence leads us into error. And it is 'a means of disowning the past,' of cutting off the present from its heritage. His mind goes back to 'the moments of happiness,' and their distinction in kind from common human satisfactions is vividly suggested by putting side by side in the same line 'a very good dinner' and 'the sudden illumination.' But what does it illumine? The poet does not say. He has had the rose-garden vision, but 'missed the meaning,' the significance of what it was designed to express. His 'approach' to that, his coming nearer to it, restores and re-stores it in a different form, which is not what we mean by 'happiness.' But he does not explain this further. He goes on to develop the idea that the meaning goes back into the pre-history of the human race. Behind 'the assurance of recorded history,' men were having these experiences of assurance and illumination: and the reverse:

> the backward half-look
> Over the shoulder, towards the primitive terror.

Terror and agony (whatever their cause) are as permanent in the pattern as assurance and ecstasy.

Going back to the imagery of sea and river, the poet weaves the ideas of the perpetual and simultaneous destruction and preservation in human experience into the metaphors. If we think of time as the sea, we can think of the moments of agony as the rocks. Our personal ones become sunken, 'covered by currents of action.' But the stark facts of the indestructible presence of these moments in the endless flux is there. 'People change and smile: but the agony abides.' The river which is within us all is also a history of such perpetual destruction and preservation. Like a great flood on the Mississippi the river of the human race preserves *itself,* but carries a cargo of wreckage and dark deeds. That river has its source in the myth of the garden where man, having been warned of 'the bitter apple' nevertheless took 'the bite in the apple.' That deed, like all the other moments of terror and agony, is permanent 'with such permanence as time has.' It stands as 'the ragged rock in the restless waters' and 'is what it always was'—the symbolic scene of the first wreck.

No 'meaning' has been revealed here. One part of the movement has ended with the faint echo of the Annunciation and the possibility of rebirth; the other with the fact of original sin and the imperfectibility of man. Approach to the meaning seems to draw all human experience of agony and illumination within the orbit of those two events. The pattern is that of a unity within which creation and destruction are perpetual and co-existent; and the pattern is always the same at any moment in the flux.

The next movement continues the exploration of the same thoughts, changing the metaphors in which they are made concrete. Man caught in time as sequence is no longer drifting in a boat or a fisherman intent on his business, he is a traveller by train or on an ocean liner. We are in the world of today. But the theme of the unity of all time in the pattern of 'reality,' and of the past existing in the present, is brought home by going back to the remote period of the Bhagavad-gita for the illustration of its eternal truth. The poet's thought jumps back over the centuries in his musing commentary. Has his 'approach to the meaning' brought him to the same conclusion reached by the Hindu religious philosophers more than two thousand years ago? In fresh metaphors he develops the concept in the sestina, 'We cannot think . . . of a future that is not liable/Like the past, to have no destination.' Sequence is endless repetition of the same 'waste, sad time.' Again the other pattern suggests itself; up or down, forwards or backwards in time, the true 'way' brings us to the present moment as the only reality.

> You cannot face it steadily, but this thing is sure,
> That time is no healer: the patient is no longer here.

This again is what Heraclitus had said about never stepping twice into the same stream. Eliot puts it in terms of a 'patient.' There is no answer to the problem of suffering in the pattern of past and future; the agony abides, though individual man still thinks of himself as escaping from the past into a new future. Time carries us along; we have the illusion of going forwards;

> While the narrowing rails slide together behind you;
> And on the deck of the drumming liner
> Watching the furrow that widens behind you

But any real development is in *consciousness* not in time.

> At nightfall, in the rigging and the aerial,
> Is a voice descanting (though not to the ear,
> The murmuring shell of time, and not in any language)

Among all the scientific means of communication we worshippers of the machine have rigged up, there is an inner voice. It sings in counterpoint to the 'faded song' of the delusion of departure and arrival. It sings 'Fare forward,' and the poet clarifies its message. It is the same truth that Krishna (one of the incarnations of Vishnu the Preserver) taught Arjuna when he hesitated to take action. He too saw two 'spheres of being,' the manifested and the unmanifested, 'which is eternally existent.' Disinterested action is the detachment from self which leads towards the higher sphere, under the 'Law of Karma.' Perhaps we may paraphrase what Eliot is saying thus: On the quality of thought and action at *this* moment depends the quality of life. Every moment is a death, an end—and a beginning. It is *this* moment which 'shall fructify in the lives of others.' But this has nothing to do with the sense of fruition which he has bracketed before with a very good dinner, or with the fruit and periodicals which are the pastimes of the journey. For to think of the fructification is to think of the future. 'Fare forward' does not mean that. It means the detachment from self of the spiritual exploration into 'another intensity.'

> O voyagers, O seamen,
> You who come to port, and you whose bodies
> Will suffer the trial and judgement of the sea,
> Or whatever event, this is your real destination.

This is to be in the sphere of existence which is 'reality': this is to be 'still and still moving.'

It is in keeping with the deep humanity which informs this whole poem that the lyric fourth movement should be this apparently simple prayer. But though so simple, it gathers up in its intercession all the 'wistful regret' for the waste sad time described in the earlier movements. The shrine stands on the promontory, the headland associated with 'the wailing warning.' It asks that a prayer should be repeated, in place of the endless repetition of the voices of the sea and of the aerial; a prayer for all sojourners in time, the drifters, the fishermen, those on conducted tours, and those who are already concerned with the law and conduct of life, but are likewise on the sea of time. Also for all those anxious worried women who wait and watch, and all those whose ships have foundered, who

> Ended their voyage on the sand, in the sea's lips
> Or in the dark throat which will not reject them
> Or wherever cannot reach them the sound of the sea
>   bell's
> Perpetual angelus.

The Lady unites all, for she is Queen of Heaven, and at the same time she is identified with humanity, earthly mother and daughter of God. 'The one Annunciation' is a perpetual angelus which transforms the calamitous annunciation into the reminder of perpetual rebirth.

The final movement creates the culminating point in the exploration which has been pursued throughout from the opening of *Burnt Norton*. What has been presented obliquely and approached through all the varied symbolism and metaphor is here given its most open statement in a climactic passage bare of all imagery. But it is prefaced by an introduction where the communication which is prayer and intercession is suddenly juxtaposed to the kinds of 'converse with spirits' which deaden the sound of the 'voice descanting' or the sea bell. One of the elements of the strong brown god in man's bloodstream is his reliance on superstition; his belief that he can descry his fate by the practice of divination, from that of the Etruscan haruspex to modern palmistry.

> Men's curiosity searches past and future
> And clings to that dimension.

Curiosity implies the desire to know, but with the suggestion of unlawful prying in the methods employed. There is the idea of using searchlights instead of 'illumination' and perhaps a hint of clinging to the rigging of the ship which will inevitably founder in the seas of time.

Then, as elsewhere in the poems, within the rhythm of a single line ('Quick, now, here, now, always—') we are out of 'that dimension' and into the description of 'the point of inter-section of the timeless/With time.' It is only the saint who can make that point his dwelling, and even he does not possess it, but is possessed by it. It is

> something given
> And taken, in a lifetime's death in love,
> Ardour and selflessness and self-surrender.

For most of us there can be none of this continuity of attain-ment, this absolute detachment from the limitation of desire.

> For most of us, there is only the unattended
> Moment, the moment in and out of time,
> The distraction fit, lost in a shaft of sunlight,
> The wild thyme unseen, or the winter lightning
> Or the waterfall, or music heard so deeply
> That it is not heard at all, but you are the music
> While the music lasts.

The moment is *unattended,* it is not ministered to and served as the sovereign value; not watched and waited for with our full attention. It is just an unexpected visitation of ecstasy, a sudden madness, as we 'lose ourselves' in the beauty of nature or of art. The central lines of the Quartets follow:

> These are only hints and guesses,
> Hints followed by guesses; and the rest
> Is prayer, observance, discipline, thought and action.
> The hint half guessed, the gift half understood, is
> Incarnation.

Eliot does not say *the* Incarnation, for the poems are not concerned with the conceptual apparatus of theology, but with the exploration of truth in the terms of human experience. The line gathers up all that we have seen and felt of that and does not go beyond it. Capitalized, Incarnation is to our Christian civilization, the ultimate symbol of the union of sense and spirit, the resolution of the paradoxes of life and death, time and the timeless; a symbol of totality, of wholeness, to which all time-experience is relative. But in the poems, it has been shown to be a *principle* active throughout the universe. The shaft of sunlight, the winter lightning, the waterfall, the scent of the wild thyme, the music, are all incarnations; that is, they are all an invisible energy manifesting itself in the phenomena of sense. And on the human level this same principle is active in the moral and emotional spheres in every experience of spiritual death and rebirth during the individual lifetime. In that symbol 'the impossible union/Of spheres of existence is actual': the turning world comes within the timeless pattern; and there is a living centre where the oppositions are reconciled and which controls 'right action.' Into those simple words are absorbed all the tumult of the river and the sea, the mournful drifting, the setting and hauling, the busy travelling, the 'seasons and rages' of the strong brown god. *Right* has many meanings which are relevant here: regulated, undeviating, not erroneous.

> And right action is freedom
> From past and future also.

It is free of the tyranny of time because, as Krishna taught, it is the disinterested action, the non-attachment which does not look for fruits. For most of us this is aim only not end, 'never here to be realised,' for 'human kind/Cannot bear very much reality.' All complexities fall away in the very moving simplicity of the next two lines, where the poet identifies himself with all men,

> Who are only undefeated
> Because we have gone on trying;

The last lines carry on the same simple, flexible movement, but they concentrate a great deal into the words.

> We, content at the last
> If our temporal reversion nourish
> (Not too far from the yew-tree)
> The life of significant soil.

On the surface 'our temporal reversion' means physical death, and reminds us of the *Burnt Norton* lyric, and of the rustic dancers in *East Coker* 'under earth/Nourishing the corn.' But this 'life of significant soil' is more than that. This is a poem about fruitfulness of action and rebirth. So our temporal reversion may mean too our whole existence on the turning world; or our return from the moments at the point of intersection to the world of time. I think all these are implied. If 'right action' can govern them they will 'fructify in the life of others.' They will have meaning, significance, and be a human part of the pattern of death and rebirth whose symbol in nature is the evergreen yew-tree planted in the churchyard.

LITTLE GIDDING

Burnt Norton is the only Quartet where the 'moment' of revelation is not linked to a Christian symbol. The rose-garden scene is a vision of an ecstasy of love, but it is man and nature which make the pattern. In *East Coker* it is the presence of the wounded surgeon that gives meaning to the moments of agony; and in *The Dry Salvages* the promise of rebirth is the moment of the Annunciation. In *Little Gidding* the fulfilment of that promise is symbolized in that 'baptism with the Holy Ghost and with fire' which is the feast of Pentecost.

Fire is the master element in the poem, and it has a fourfold aspect: as the emblem of destruction, of purification, of illumination, and of the divine love itself. Little Gidding was the site of an Anglican religious community founded in 1625. The community was broken up in 1647, but the ruined chapel rebuilt in the nineteenth century. It is a visit to this chapel which is the starting point of the poem. Little Gidding was associated with the English civil war, and the poet is writing in the midst of a greater war. As in *East Coker,* there is a sense of the passionate identification of the poet with his country's experience, as well as the detached, but also impassioned, exploration of the total meaning of that experience.

Unlike the other poems it opens with a moment of kindling illumination. It is a day of 'midwinter spring,' and though its details suggest such a day 'in time's covenant,' it is 'not in the scheme of generation.' It is the precise antithesis to the scene in *East Coker.* Everything refracts and radiates light. Instead of 'dark in the afternoon,' 'a glare that is blindness'; instead of the haze of sultry heat, 'the brief sun flames the ice'; instead of the sense of hypnotic paralysis, 'the soul's sap quivers.' Again, in the place of the destructive fire and ice, the sun and frost blend in perfect harmony 'in windless cold that is the heart's heat.' The snow itself is 'blossom.' The poet ends the description of the glowing intensity with the question:

> Where is the summer, the unimaginable
> Zero summer?

If the union of spring and winter has this glory, what can the full consciousness and complete union of opposites be?

Although 'suspended in time,' we are on the actual road to Little Gidding, and the details of the scene are there; the hedges, which in May will be white 'with voluptuary sweetness,' the pig-sty, the dull façade and the tombstone. But this lane insists on the direction to the chapel, not the village. This is 'the end of the journey,' whether the traveller is Charles I after

his defeat at Naseby, or a modern tourist. Little Gidding itself
is now only a shell or husk, and the purpose or end of the
journey there breaks forth only if what you 'figured' becomes
transfigured and 'is altered in fulfilment.' *Altered* must be
heard in the ear as well as read by the eye. It is 'the world's
end,' the end of the purely temporal, just as death is the end
for so many during the war:

> some at the sea jaws,
> Or over a dark lake, in a desert or a city—

But this experience is here in this actual chapel.

'If you came this way,' now gathers in all that 'the way' has
meant during the course of the poems. The experience is the
same always. 'You would have to put off/Sense and notion'—
all the joy of 'voluptuary sweetness,' the merely opinionated,
the ingenious counters of common exchange. It is useless too
to come to Little Gidding in the spirit of the historical re-
searcher verifying his scholarship or the journalist writing up
a story. 'You are here to kneel/Where prayer has been valid.'
And prayer means the sense of living relationship with the
timeless reality which drew together the original community at
Little Gidding. And it means too the sense of living relationship
with those men, for 'the communication/Of the dead is tongued
with fire beyond the language of the living.' The reaching of
'the point of intersection' is 'now and in England,' but it
is also nowhere, never and always.

In the second movement, 'England and nowhere,' the particular and the general, the themes and symbols of the other
Quartets as well as new material, are woven into a fresh and
haunting fabric of words. The lyric seems to confound
Heraclitus: 'Fire lives in the death of air; air lives in the death

of fire; water lives in the death of earth and earth lives in the death of water.' Here there is no creative strife among the elements. They are destructive only and they cancel out to nothingness. The scene of wartime desolation represents the death of everything creative that the elements have represented in the nature of man. Time takes away life and gives no new birth. The roses of *Burnt Norton* are 'ash on an old man's sleeve'; the dust is lit by no shaft of sunlight. Houses die but they do not live, 'old stone to new buildings.' Water and sand are both dead, and instead of 'significant' soil,

> The parched eviscerate soil
> Gapes at the vanity of toil

There is succession without renewal; end without beginning; suspension without transfiguration. All the living patterns in the world of nature and those created as the work of man's hands have disintegrated with no hope of resurrection. The laughter of the hidden children becomes the derision of the elements at man's forgetfulness and denial of the foundations of his being, and of the central truth which any chapel commemorates.

> Water and fire deride
> The sacrifice that we denied.
> Water and fire shall rot
> The marred foundations we forgot,
> Of sanctuary and choir.

What is left after this holocaust of destruction? The answer is given in the wonderful dream sequence that follows. The conversation between the spirit from purgatory and the poet himself in the London dawn after an air-raid—'two worlds become much like each other'—inevitably recalls Dante. The verse too is a rhythmical variation of a *terza rima,* and one feels that this must be one of those occasions when the poetry realized itself first as a particular rhythm before it reached expression in words, so deeply does the movement flow in and under the verbal surface.

The scene is the antithesis of the Pentecostal symbols. The dove becomes the airplane; the tongues of flame those of the guns; the 'rushing mighty wind' that of the 'urban dawn' blowing the 'metal leaves' of the fragments of shrapnel over the asphalt. The poet as air-raid warden patrols the streets, and his soul meets 'a familiar compound ghost,' a familiar spirit 'both intimate and unidentifiable,' composed of all the dead poets who have become a part of himself. The ghost is the poetic parallel to the Holy Ghost; for the 'tongue' of poetry is likewise communication, interpretation, illumination. The poet's soul and the ghost, 'too strange to each other for mis-understanding,' for the squabbles and mis-readings of criticism have no place here, are 'in concord' in another moment of 'intersection': 'we trod the pavement in a dead patrol.' The ghost will not speak to him of 'thought and theory' in poetry, for that is a matter of continual ends and beginnings:

> Last season's fruit is eaten
> And the fullfed beast shall kick the empty pail.

But since it is the concern of the poet to 'learn to use words' to interpret and illumine life to others, he will reveal in poetry the reality of old age to the poet, just as to all other men. The lines need no interpretation.

> Let me disclose the gifts reserved for age
> To set a crown upon your lifetime's effort.
> First, the cold friction of expiring sense
> Without enchantment, offering no promise
> But bitter tastelessness of shadow fruit
> As body and soul begin to fall asunder.
> Second, the conscious impotence of rage
> At human folly, and the laceration
> Of laughter at what ceases to amuse.

And last, the rending pain of re-enactment
　　Of all that you have done, and been; the shame
　　Of motives late revealed, and the awareness
Of things ill done and done to others' harm
　　Which once you took for exercise of virtue.
　　Then fools' approval stings, and honour stains.
From wrong to wrong the exasperated spirit
　　Proceeds,

Again, with the pause of a comma only, comes the possibility of moving into the other dimension. Not less torment, but a torment within the creative pattern. Old age in time can be only bodily decay, bitterness, and the torture of memory,

　　　　　　　　　unless restored by that refining fire
　　Where you must move in measure, like a dancer.

The fire of illumination of the opening of the poem is not enough. That is the 'stillness.' But there must also be the 'faring forward' into the intensity of the purifying fire, detached from self, and part of the dance controlled from the still point. The 'measure' of the dance is placed not only against the raging, unquiet spirit of old age, but also against the actual scene of the 'dead patrol' and the windblown, rattling leaves. The 'disfigured street' is opposed to the way of transfiguration in the figure of the dance. We can guess that the 'kind of valediction' the ghost gave was that of *The Dry Salvages* 'not fare well,/But fare forward.'

　　The tone now changes completely and the voice is that which speaks throughout the poems in discursive exploratory analysis; but it has more assurance and certainty here. It tells of the two creative kinds of love, attachment and detachment and of the unflowering indifference. Both attachment and detachment are 'nettles,' but they are within the rhythm of birth and death. Detachment is the disinterested love, hence the 'right action' which gives freedom from time. Memory brings it, for in it we can see the past without personal involvement in it, and *use* it to enrich the spiritual significance of the present. History may be servitude, because it may 'impose a pattern' of mere traditionalism, just as patriotism may be only a kind of family loyalty. Detachment does not lose personal love in indifference, it absorbs it into something larger.

> See, now they vanish,
> The faces and places, with the self which, as it could,
>   loved them,
> To become renewed, transfigured, in another pattern.

This is developed in a change of rhythm. Little Gidding reminds the poet of the religious and political civil war and of the men who fought it. He dwells on these 'ghosts,' not to support the Royalist cause, or that of Milton, or to pretend that there is any value in arguing the rights and wrongs of the struggle. Both sides now

> Accept the constitution of silence
> And are folded in a single party.

The party is that which fights to keep alive the values of the spirit, and the symbol they leave is the reminder that detachment is a 'field of action' where this struggle is ended only in death. The whole passage is framed in two allusions from the writings of the fourteenth century mystic, Dame Julian of Norwich. In 'shewings' she received, a voice said to her 'Sin is behovable (necessary) but all shall be well . . . and all manner of thing shall be well.' And again the voice said: 'I am Ground of thy Beseeching,' which was interpreted to her to mean Love. The 'field of action' therefore, and the motive force in this spiritual strife is love.

If these passages seem a little soft and over-simplified, the next lyric at once dispels the idea of any easy solution. As the gentle tenderness of the fourth movement of *The Dry Salvages* has something of the same quality as that in *Burnt Norton,* so this matches the tone of the Good Friday lyric in *East Coker* in its stern acceptance of the attitude 'requiring, pointing to the agony/of death and birth.' There is the same compression of language and intricate correspondences, but it has greater intensity and explosive force, and for the first time there is the overt use of the terms of sin and redemption.

The central symbol is the implicit reference to the descent of the Holy Ghost at the baptism of Christ, and of the tongues of flame which inspired the disciples so that they 'began to speak with other tongues as the Spirit gave them utterance.' We should also remember that the Jewish Pentecost is the celebration of the giving of the law to the Israelites, and that the English name for it is Whit (white) Sunday. Against all these implicit oppositions, 'the dark dove with the flickering tongue' descends in destructive wrath and 'breaks the air/With flame of incandescent terror.' The utterance from *its* tongues of flame is the declaration of 'the one discharge from sin and error.' *Discharge* explodes into many meanings. The message of the tongues of flame is that *one* way of relieving the burden of our own sin is by projecting it in hatred of others; or again one way to discharge a debt is on the principle of revenge. Again the release of the bomb or the gun is one form of resolving a tension. 'Tongues' too, in wartime are always busy saying that hate is justified. But there is another message from the tongues saying:

> The only hope, or else despair
>   Lies in the choice of pyre or pyre—
>   To be redeemed from fire by fire.

Unless we are to despair and choose the fires of destruction and damnation—and it is a matter of man's *choice*—there is no other way than to accept our debt of sin and error and discharge it through the fire of purgatory. We shall then be discharged of it, and the dove, though coming no less as 'flame of incandescent terror' is the redeeming fire of God.

> Who then devised the torment? Love.

I think *devised,* in addition to its common use, carries a meaning from the derivation linking it with *divide.* The whole positive weight behind the love in relation to the torment is brought out by the accentuation, and its singleness. That creative and destructive fires can be all part of one process, and that their opposition is 'conquered and reconciled' in the symbolic pattern of redemption personified in the Name, is unrecognized:

> Love is the unfamiliar Name
> Behind the hands that wove
> The intolerable shirt of flame
> Which human power cannot remove.

Hercules could not tear off the poisoned Nessus shirt which was supposed to preserve human love forever, so in his agony he built a pyre on which his mortal body burned and his divine element ascended to Olympus. Again though it is man's hands that have woven the unendurable shirt of flame of his own desires, and the 'incandescent terror' of war, the divine love is also an 'intolerable shirt of flame.' But behind man's hands are those of the wounded surgeon showing how pain can heal.

> We only live, only suspire
> Consumed by either fire or fire.

Each one of us has the choice between the fires of destruction (*suspire* brings the memory of the sighs of the inhabitants of the Inferno) or the burning away of self-love on the sacrificial pyre, whose consuming fires bring a promised consummation.

In these last lines, where everything becomes 'the condition of fire,' the 'tongues' descend from Heraclitus to Dante and from both to the poet of today so much fired by each.

The opening of the final movement restates the central theme of the continuity and co-existence of death and rebirth in the metaphor of beginning and ending. Then the ever-existing pattern of vital relationships alive in every moment is suggested by the analogy of a sentence that is 'right.' That too contains all the essentials of a vital society. 'Every word is at home,/Taking its place to support the others,' which suggests the human family. The words unite past and present, 'an easy commerce of the old and the new.' They are of all kinds, and exist in a coherent, harmonious pattern, 'the complete consort dancing together.' Writing and living then converge in the reminder that every phrase and every moment is an end and a beginning. Any action is a step towards physical death, but physical death is unreal in the changeless pattern. The dead are alive in the present, their actions can be reborn in us. Hence the true pattern of history is not a sequence in time, but is a 'familiar compound ghost' of the spiritual values which have made a people, 'a pattern of timeless moments.' These exist apart from the cycle in which night follows day and winter summer:

> So, while the light fails
> On a winter's afternoon, in a secluded chapel
> History is now and England.

A disembodied voice in the quiet chapel seems to speak the next line, poised by itself before the finale begins.

With the drawing of this Love and the voice of this Calling [19]

It gathers into itself the opening scene of love in the rose-garden and the calling of the bird; all the moments of insight and all that the living tongues of the past have declared; and the vocation of the poet.

The conclusion weaves together the main symbols and metaphors of the four poems and the truths they embody, into a new whole.

> We shall not cease from exploration
> And the end of all our exploring
> Will be to arrive where we started
> And know the place for the first time.
> Through the unknown, remembered gate
> When the last of earth left to discover
> Is that which was the beginning;
> At the source of the longest river
> The voice of the hidden waterfall
> And the children in the apple-tree
> Not known, because not looked for
> But heard, half-heard, in the stillness
> Between two waves of the sea.
> Quick now, here, now, always—
> A condition of complete simplicity
> (Costing not less than everything)
> And all shall be well and
> All manner of thing shall be well
> When the tongues of flame are in-folded
> Into the crowned knot of fire
> And the fire and the rose are one.

First, all the metaphors relating man's nature and the natural world are recapitulated and blended. Exploration is endless, but all exploring into further spiritual intensity and communion will bring us back to the worlds of nature and man, the rose-garden, to find it 'renewed, transfigured in another pattern.' The remembered gate into 'our first world' leads, unknown, to

---

[19] It is a quotation from *The Cloud of Unknowing*, an anonymous mystical work of the fourteenth century.

'that which was the beginning.' It leads to the myth of the Garden of Eden and its river of life flowing from the hidden waterfall, 'and the children in the apple-tree.' 'The bitter apple and the bite in the apple' was not known before under that image, but 'the ragged rock in the restless waters' is now transformed. It becomes an image holding a promise of growth and fruition, for 'heard, half-heard, in the stillness,/Between two waves of the sea,' is the bell of the angelus and 'the hint half guessed, the gift half understood.'

Here the symbolic 'exploration' by means of natural imagery ends, and the next lines are purely abstract. They blend into a unity the particular spiritual reality given by the voice and the calling in each poem. The bird's call told of the eternal presence of the point of intersection: 'Quick, now, here, now, always—.' *East Coker* revealed that the only timeless wisdom is humility: 'a condition of complete simplicity.' *The Dry Salvages* told of the vocation of the saint 'a lifetime's death in love': '(Costing not less than everything.)' In *Little Gidding* strife and sin and death are conquered by the voice which says 'All shall be well.' This leads into the final intricate symbol of the ultimate vision, drawing in images and associations from the rest of the poem and irradiating them with new illumination. The 'ghost' from purgatory in the dark dawn had disclosed ironically the 'gifts' which the time-world brings 'to set a crown upon your lifetime's efforts.' The final revelation is of 'the gift half understood' of the timeless pattern now disclosed and glittering out of heart of light. All conflicts are conquered by the crowned kingship of love. All the 'tongues' which have spoken for the spirit of man are 'folded into a single party.' All the strands of the opposites are reconciled in the lover's knot [20] woven from the fires. Flame becomes flower. Nature and spirit, the rose-garden and the chapel, are one.

---

[20] The author of *The Cloud of Unknowing* says that renunciation and humility 'will at the last help thee to knit a ghostly knot of burning love betwixt thee and thy God in ghostly one head.'

And this finale with its crowning symbol, in which everything has 'come together,' in which all that has passed is fused and intertwined into this easy flow and this glowing intensity, is poetic art. The poems are the creation of that union of sense and spirit which issues in living language interpreting the experience of living. They are the crown of a lifetime's effort to get the better of words, to make them stay still and yet dance together in complete consort. For the poet, maybe, mostly a matter of 'the intolerable wrestle with words and meanings,' but ending in that sole work of man's hands which is changelessly enduring and harmonious, the form and pattern of a work of art.

CHAPTER XI

❖❖❖

'The Voice of This Calling'

> The enduring is no substitute for the transient,
> Neither one for the other. But the abstract conception
> Of private experience at its greatest intensity
> Becoming universal, which we call 'poetry,'
> May be affirmed in verse.
>
> T. S. ELIOT. A Note on War Poetry

ELIOT'S mature poetic faith is as closely woven into the anatomy of *Four Quartets* as his religious faith. Throughout the poems an analogy between the writing of poetry and the living of life is sustained and developed. The poems are about the nature of the universe, of its two inter-relating spheres of existence as turning world and eternal pattern, as the transient and the enduring, and of the way the creative man's life is inextricably involved in both. But they include too the matter of the nature of poetic art, of its existence as sequence and as unity; of the poet as transient but the work as enduring; of the relation of the poet to his medium; and of his function in the community.

In his lecture on Yeats, Eliot said: 'It is my experience that towards middle age a man has three choices: to stop writing altogether, to repeat himself with perhaps an increasing skill of virtuosity, or by taking thought to adapt himself to middle age and find a different way of working.' This last is the difficult task, because 'maturing as a poet means maturing as the whole man, experiencing new emotions appropriate to one's age, and with the same intensity as the emotion of youth.' And these feelings are not merely a new set of conditions: 'the

201

interesting feelings of age are not just different feelings; they are feelings into which the feelings of youth are integrated.'

Integration is central to all Eliot's ideas of life and of poetry. The concept in which both are grounded is that of a pattern of creative order. His review of *Ulysses* hailed the method of myth as a way of ordering, of giving shape and significance to vision, and when *mythos* and *logos* have become inseparable it is the same. It is the theme behind everything he has written in both poetry and prose. Perhaps it is natural that in view of the appalling *dis*order of the modern world, its greatest writers should have taken the search for order as their quest. Among writers in English, Yeats, Joyce and Eliot, each in his own way, has created the progress of that exploration. Each has sought for the secret of totality of being, for some pattern of relationships which shall, as it were, hold man and men together in a universe where, more and more, the image of fractured atoms whirled in senseless circuit conquers all. Yeats failed to create any ordered world vision in his poetry. In *A Vision*, his complicated 'system' tried to give some kind of schematization to experience, and it is perhaps of psychological interest that his great wheel, and phases of the moon, and cones and gyres and four faculties and four principles are obviously 'mandala' forms of psychic experience. But he could not produce in poetic or dramatic form anything in the way of an ordered cosmogony, and he remains a poet of magnificent achievement in individual examples of lyric and meditation. Like Eliot, however, Yeats (though he found no controlling image for it) felt passionately that the only orders discovered and pursued in the civilization of today are the ever-extended 'metalled roads' of *imposed* orders—scientific classification and measurement in the world of knowledge; mechanization in the world of industry; international bondage in the world of finance; bureaucracy or totalitarianism in the world of government. And Yeats too felt that outside of these orders imposed upon the individual from without, yet woven by his own hands into a shirt of chain-mail about him, the life of the average man becomes ever more purposeless, more confined, more 'distracted' and more 'empty of meaning.'

Against all this Eliot sees on the one hand, the world of natural order, with its great organic cycles of birth-death, winter-summer, day-night, and its great harmonious tensions of energy holding all together in pattern. This is the cycle and pattern which Joyce took as his controlling symbol in *Finnegans Wake*. The title suggests that human life is one vast funeral, and yet a matter of rejoicing, since life and death, joy and sorrow, are inextricably one. Moreover the cycle of historical experience, and the river of life, and man himself as the microcosm of both, are all inexhaustible, and their contemplation is sufficient for the human imagination.

But to Eliot such experience and such contemplation are inadequate. Natural law is meaningless, unless complemented and completed by spiritual law, and these two creative 'spheres' become united in the symbol of Incarnation. Capitalized, it is the ultimate symbol of revelation, illumination, transfiguration. But it is also the process at work in all man's true experiences of self-fulfilment. On earth, in religious experience, it has its highest reflection in the symbol of the saint, which Eliot has used in one of his plays. In the secular world its revelation is the presence of art, and that is the symbol which he chose as the title of *Four Quartets*. On the musical side perhaps we can expand and extend its overtones to include 'the music of the spheres!' But Eliot is poet and his own creative sphere is that of poetry. The relation of poetry to the central symbol is of a very precise kind. The ultimate revelation is the image of communication by *speech:* the Word. Hence in the world of human communication by speech, poetry is its most perfect counterpart; the revelation and illumination and transfiguration of life through the word.

This cannot be accomplished by the poet without a discipline parallel to that practiced in the dedication to the life of religious devotion. It is only by the loss of self in his art that the poet's consciousness is directed, ordered, focussed, intensified, and thus made ever more powerful in the diffusion of its energy beyond itself. 'One is prepared for art when one has ceased to be interested in one's own emotions except as material . . . Personal emotion, personal experience is extended and completed in something impersonal—not in the sense of something divorced from personal experience and passion. No good poetry is the latter . . . Not our feelings, but the pattern we make of our feelings is the centre of value.' [1] This was written in 1924, but Eliot's theory and practice of poetry have been consistent throughout his life. The things he was actively engaged in battling for when he started writing are the things he continues to battle for, but the feelings and the patterns made of the feelings have steadily changed and deepened.

He has always been master of what, in a rare lapse into the hideous language of modern abstraction, he has called the 'objective correlative.' In *Prufrock* that creation of thinking into feeling, of projecting the inner life in terms of weather and scenery and rooms and gestures and disease and sounds and textures, seemed already complete. With age he has lost none of that richness of sensibility, but it has been expanded to cover wider areas of experience. And in addition to this he has developed a new method of direct philosophical analysis in poetic form, and has infolded the two into a poetry of contemplation which is as sensuous as it is intellectual. The subject contemplated is pattern; a pattern which, the further it is explored in any direction, up or down, inwards or outwards, forward or back, is found to be one vast system of dynamic ordered relationships. And so it is with the poetry itself. It

[1] T. S. Eliot. Introduction to *Le Serpent* by Paul Valery.

has all the qualities alive in the earlier poetry; acuteness of sensibility, structural strength and elasticity, rhythmical variation, absorption of the past and its recreation into new poetic life. But whereas in the early poems these qualities had often to be asserted through a *dislocation* of language, in *Four Quartets* they are knit into a perfect articulation of sound and movement and meaning. Instead of dramatic clashes and startling associations and references which require constant elucidation from outside the poems, the language itself penetrates more and more deeply into the structure, the *word* becomes more and more loaded with meaning. It is squeezed and squeezed of every drop of its juice. It is ex-pression at its fullest.

The 'familiar compound ghost' said of poets:

> our concern was speech, and speech impelled us
> To purify the dialect of the tribe
> And urge the mind to aftersight and foresight . . .

The purification and the replenishment of the English language is a continuous process in Eliot's poetry, and we might extend his description of the phrase or sentence that is 'right' very widely.

> (where every word is at home,
> Taking its place to support the others,
> The word neither diffident nor ostentatious,
> An easy commerce of the old and the new,
> The common word exact without vulgarity,
> The formal word precise but not pedantic,
> The complete consort dancing together)

But the ghost added that speech compels the poet 'to urge the mind to aftersight and foresight.' The dialect of the tribe is inextricably interwoven with the life of its members and with life in general. The life of the word extends beyond itself, not only backwards into the family history of the language, not only around itself in its context, and from there in linked relationships to other parts of the poetic pattern, but to a human context. 'The complete consort dancing together' is not only the organic affinity of the words in the poetic structure, it is also the inter-relationship and inseparability of poetry and life. When the poet is at work, says Eliot, 'he is no more concerned with the social consequences than the scientist in his laboratory—though without the context of use to society, neither the writer nor the scientist could have the conviction which sustains him.' [2]

The poet's own immediate task is to bring all the depth and intensity of his own full consciousness to a verbal surface: the reader, starting from the surface, penetrates gradually to the full consciousness beneath. Poetry is thus both act and instrument. It is the poet's tongue speaking 'a language of enticement' to his fellow men, and urging them, through a sharing of his speech to share his own aftersight, foresight and insight.

> In expressing what other people feel he is also changing the feeling by making it more conscious; he is making people more aware of what they feel already, and therefore teaching them something about themselves. But he is not merely a more conscious person than the others; he is also individually different from other people and from other poets too, and can make his readers share consciously in new feelings which they had not experienced before.[3]

In *Four Quartets* the poet is trying to awaken the consciousness of his age to its situation. He does not urge the tribe to

[2] *The Music of Poetry.*
[3] 'The Social Function of Poetry.' *The Adelphi.* July-September 1945.

a religious and political viewpoint by preaching or argument, he urges them to sight through vision.

Nothing could be clearer than the vision of western civilization he creates. We see man, having solved all the problems 'confronting the builder of bridges,' living among his metalled roads, his ocean liners, his aerials, his Directory of Directors. He 'tends to forget' the strong brown god, the demonic chthonic powers by which he may be driven, and who use 'the worshippers of the machine' for their own purposes; always 'watching and waiting,' and finally declaring themselves in the tongues of incandescent terror.[4] On the other side, neither in city nor in village is there a society 'keeping the rhythm in their dancing, as in their living' in an ordered 'concorde.' Instead, the individual is detached, a whirling bit of paper, or wandering in a bramble or a grimpen with no secure foothold, or lying awake trying to unweave, unwind, unravel, the tangle of its fate. And along with the busy travelling along material ways, the inorganic metalled roads, or the helpless unrelatedness of anxious insecurity, is the refusal to face any experience of the inner life—the torpor, the apathy, the 'silent funeral'; or what in prose Eliot has called 'the invincible sluggishness of imagination,' which paralyzes all movement, and repudiates all responsibility.

And over against these ways, all leading one way or another to death, the poet sets the creative pattern whose centre is life and peace; but whose way is never that of peace but always a sword. 'There is only the fight to recover what has been lost/And found and lost again and again.' The parallel with the poet and his medium is exact: the achievement, the stillness,

---

[4] 'The old religions with their ridiculous—and horrible symbols, are not born out of the blue, but out of this very human soul that lives in us at this moment . . . At any time they may break in upon us with destructive force, in the form of mass-suggestion, for example, against which the individual is defenceless. Our frightful Gods have only changed their names.' Jung. *Two Essays on Analytical Psychology*, p. 223.

those moments when the sense of 'the complete consort dancing together' is felt as a reality; but the way, the actual moving, always the struggle:

> With shabby equipment always deteriorating
> In the general mess of imprecision of feeling,
> Undisciplined squads of emotion.

The revelation of all this to the tribe, to make society and the individual share his own consciousness of it, is the poet's aim. And that again is another fight. Eliot has said [5] that it is inevitable that the man of letters should always be 'in a certain sense in opposition. He should be jealous to preserve the tradition of the culture of his people and of Europe: but in so doing he must constantly find himself opposed to current tendencies and popular values. All great literature is, in one aspect, a criticism . . . of the society in which the author lives. If he is not to criticize, he must remain silent.' Eliot's criticism probes very deep. Certainly no poet of any age has ever revealed the dilemma and disease of his own times more surely. No one except those committed to some aspect of the new paganism as a positive creed is likely to disagree with his diagnosis of the failure of western civilization in terms of misdirection, indirection and inertia. It is Eliot's insistence in his prose works on the acceptance of the letter of Christian dogma as the only way of salvation which large numbers of the tribe find a difficult medicine to swallow. It does not have to be swallowed in his poetry, since the poetry is never polemical and propagandist (except in the choruses to *The Rock*.) The poetry is the affirmation in verse of 'private experience at its greatest intensity/Becoming universal.' It is the progress of an individual personality relating itself to its total environment. It contains almost as much doubt as belief, and emotional ac-

[5] In an unpublished radio address given in October 1944 (Eliot House Collection. Harvard).

ceptance of it is certainly not confined to churchmen. Since it is concerned with symbols, it can be interpreted in any terms of human experience acceptable to the reader. Indeed the poetry is in some ways a flat contradiction of the prose position. In prose Eliot has declared stubbornly that the spirit killeth but the letter giveth life: also that the acceptance of dogma precedes emotional acceptance of Christian truths and that though intellectual conviction may come late it comes inevitably 'without violence to honesty and nature.' The only possible answer to that is that to a very great number of thinking people it does not. To these it appears that dogmatic Christianity demands the acceptance as *facts,* of 'revelation' which, while it may contain symbolically the deepest human truth, has been confined to no special period and to no special part of the map. Moreover that if a new positive 'religious' attitude is to be able to combat the new positive paganism, it cannot remain frozen and stereotyped in its traditional moulds, but must be refreshed and replenished from some new spring of symbolic interpretation.

While Eliot the prose writer asserts that heresy is diabolic and Catholic theology immutable, Eliot the poet provides us with just that refreshment and replenishment of symbolic approach which gives new meaning to old truths and reawakens the imagination to new growth. Its centre is Christianity, the traditional form of western culture, but a Christianity accepting its roots in cultures much older than itself, and recognizing itself not only in Dante and St. John of the Cross, but in age-old 'pagan' symbols of the vitality of water, of fire, of earth, and age-old concepts of the communion and relatedness of the worlds of sense and of spirit; of the supersession of guilt by an understanding of the process of symbolic death and rebirth; and of the way of 'detachment' and contemplation as a path to the kingdom of God within. All this, and the truth that 'history is a pattern of timeless moments,' and all the explorations into self-surrender and 'right action' which have led to that conclusion, provide 'revelation' indeed of profound realities, but realities whose acceptance does no violence to 'honesty and nature' and requires no supernatural sanctions. Eliot's prose sayings and his Anglo-Catholicism have perhaps blinded critics to the completely catholic, that is, universal character of his vision; to how 'at home' his conclusions are in *any* pattern of harmonious living; and how they strike home to the common roots of social and personal disorder at all times and among all peoples.

But from the point of view of 'use to society,' poetry itself can do no more towards translating revelation and insight into action than the dream image in the life of the dreamer. Action is a matter of the will. But just as the dream image *reveals* the psychic situation in sensuous form and presents it to the conscious mind, so does the work of the poet. Jung's theory is that just as the personal dream is a message from the unconscious of the personal need of the individual, so the great artist experiences and then creates in his particular art-form those archetypes of which his whole age is most in need.

> Being essentially the instrument for his work, he is subordinate to it, and we have no reason for expecting him to interpret it for us. He has done the best that in him lies by giving it form, and he must leave interpretation to others and to the future. A great work of art is like a dream . . . it does not explain itself and is never unequivocal. A dream never says: 'you ought,' or: 'This is the truth.' It presents an image . . . To grasp its meaning, we must allow it to shape us as it once shaped the artist. Then we understand the nature of his experience. We see . . . that he has penetrated to that matrix of life in which all men are imbedded, which imparts a common rhythm to all human existence, and allows the human individual to communicate his feeling and his striving to mankind as a whole.[6]

[6] 'Psychology and Literature.' *Modern Man in Search of a Soul*, p. 198.

Eliot says in *East Coker* that the poet's fight today, for both his language and his values, is under conditions 'that seem unpropitious.' There is perhaps another layer of meaning to the title of *Four Quartets* in the sense that the poet's area of resonance nowadays can be only that of chamber-music, and his audience correspondingly small. Matthew Arnold declared that 'for the creation of a master-work of literature two 'powers must concur, the power of the man and the power of the moment.' But this is inexact. The moment may be propitious or unpropitious for the artist, but the work of art stands secure in its own life not in that of the society in which it is produced. Great works of art have been produced as often when the artist was in active revolt from his age as when he was in harmony with its accepted faith. It is not the creation of the work but its acceptance by society which demands the concurrence of the man and the moment. For it is true that the communication of the power of the master-work to others rests on conditions in society over which the artist has no control and which, in his own age or in any other age, may muffle his voice and make the complex harmony of his music sound like that of 'the weak pipe and the little drum.'

When Eliot began to write, it was inevitable that his poetry should be 'undecipherable' to the reading public. The speech of the tribe had become impoverished, atrophied, inarticulate. Hence the return to some of the sources of its lost life, to the language of symbol, the logic of the imagination, made it appear a stranger, whose unfamiliarity must be repudiated. A generation of readers and critics and teachers, and of other poets writing in the same language, has done much to reawaken consciousness, and to widen the area over which the music can be heard. As to the fight for his values, all the poet can do in his art is to present them as poetry. 'The rest is not our business.' Eliot summed up that matter in his comment on Yeats:

Born into a world in which the doctrine of 'art for art's sake' was generally accepted, and living on into one in which art has been asked to be instrumental to social purposes, he held firmly to the right view which is between these, though not in any way a compromise between them, and showed that an artist, by serving his art with entire integrity, is at the same time rendering the greatest service he can to his own nation and to the whole world.

That service Eliot's adopted nation has recognized by the highest honour it could bestow, the Order of Merit. This is surely as it should be, for Eliot has united himself with his nation and its struggles and has given it his love. But in the greater realm of art, as he has said, 'there is no competition.' There is only the struggle for integrity, the honest service of the whole man towards the mastery of integration; the integration of life and words, of past and present, of words themselves into the new wholeness of a poem. In the only passage in which Eliot 'speaks out' about the dignity and glory of his calling, he transmutes this abstract 'integration' into the sense world where poetry exists. From the disorder of practical living and dying, the flux of being, the many voices, the general mess, 'spring' the words which renew and transfigure into pattern, and which embody the rhythm and order of creation.

Out of the meaningless practical shapes of all that is
    living or lifeless
Joined with the artist's eye, new life, new form, new
    colour.
Out of the sea of sound the life of music,
Out of the slimy mud of words, out of the sleet and
    hail of verbal imprecisions,
Approximate thoughts and feelings, words that have
    taken the place of thoughts and feelings,
There spring the perfect order of speech, and the
    beauty of incantation.

Bibliography

BIBLIOGRAPHY

Gradner, Helen *The Art of T. S. Eliot* Dutton. 1950

Kenner, Hugh *The Invisible Poet. T. S. Eliot* McDowell, Obolensky. 1959

Maxwell, D. E. S. *The Poetry of T. S. Eliot* London. Routledge and Kegan Paul. 1952

Matthiessen, F. O. and Barber, C. L. *The Achievement of T. S. Eliot* Oxford University Press. 1958

Mesterton, Erik *The Waste Land,* some commentaries, Chicago. The Argus Book Shop. 1943

Preston, Raymond *Four Quartets' Rehearsed* Sheed and Ward. 1946

Smith, Grover *T. S. Eliot's Poetry and Plays* University of Chicago. 1956

Williamson, George *A Reader's Guide to T. S. Eliot* Noonday Press. 1957

Wilson, Frank *Six Essays on the Development of T. S. Eliot* London. The Fortune Press. 1948

Rajan, B. (editor) *T. S. Eliot, a study of his writings by several hands.* Funk and Wagnalls. 1948

Unger, L. *T. S. Eliot. A selected critique* Rinehart. 1948

March, R. and Tambimuttu *T. S. Eliot. A symposium for his sixtieth birthday* Regnery. 1949

Braybrooke, Neville *T. S. Eliot. A symposium for his seventieth birthday.* Farrar, Strauss and Cudahy. 1958